Flipping Out

April Adams

Published by Lechner Syndications

www.lechnersyndications.com

ISBN 13: 978-1-927794-00-5

"There are no shortcuts to any place worth going."

— Beverly Sills

.

CONTENTS

APRIL ADAMS

CHAPTER 1: THE SQUAD

"Well, girls, as you can see, our group is getting smaller."

No kidding, Kelley thought.

Nadia, Jamie, and Kelley sat on the balance beam ready for their pre-practice pep-and-prep talk with Coach Judi.

Nadia cradled her smartphone in her hands. A video played of Russian gymnast Aliya Mustafina's Olympic gold-winning uneven bars routine.

"She even has style on bars," Nadia muttered under her breath. She'd become obsessed with her own artistic scores ever since she'd placed second across the board—except for vault—at Regionals.

Kelley and Jamie shared a headset, listening to the Beyonce song that Kelley was hoping to use for her floor routine at Nationals. She was tired of the country music line dancing choreography she'd used at Optionals and Regionals—even if it had been a crowd-pleaser. She wanted something that fit her personality and the do-si-do wasn't cutting it.

The girls still wore their team colors to practice every day—fuchsia black, and silver—but it was getting hard to keep up squad spirit. Of the original five members, only three were left.

"I have to say—," Nadia began.

Jamie and Kelley exchanged a look that clearly said, "Here it comes." Nadia could be direct at best.

"…I always thought it would be you who dropped out, Kelley,"

1

Nadia twisted into a lower-back stretch. "Sara and Bethany were so die-hard. You have so many other interests."

A few weeks ago, this comment would have made Kelley cry, but she understood Nadia better now.

"Maybe that's why the pressure got to them," Kelley replied. "No down time."

"Who would have thought NOT focusing on gymnastics would be the thing that kept you sane?" Nadia wondered.

"I think you mean that as a compliment?" Jamie asked.

Nadia nodded impatiently. "Can't you tell?" The hint of a smile betrayed her softer side.

Kelley grinned.

"Does that mean *you're* about to lose it?" she asked. "You don't do anything *except* focus on gym."

"Don't hold your breath," Nadia replied, as she refreshed her video.

Things had always been tense between Nadia and Kelley—a strange cold war between the hyper-serious and slightly-less-than-hyper serious. But lately, Nadia needed Kelley's dance training to help her improve on artistry, so Nadia couldn't be too harsh when Kelley was late to practice because of a soccer game or dance workshop.

Judi clapped her hands to get their attention. Jamie slipped her iPod into the pocket of her warm-up suit.

"Now that Sara is on a medical break," Judi began, "and Bethany has decided not to compete at Nationals, we've had to allow one more gymnast to work out with our team. As you know we'll need four total to compete for the all-around team medals and I want my squad to be competitive."

Nadia looked up from her smartphone, hiding any trace of emotion.

"Where did you find her?" she asked, sitting up even taller.

"Seattle Gym Club," said Judi.

"Hmpf," Nadia replied.

"That's great!" said Jamie. "They placed silver in the all-around at Nationals last year. They have a really strong record."

"It's not that short girl from Regionals with the atrocious kips, is it?" Nadia asked. "She'll just bring us down."

Judi frowned. "I'm afraid you'll all just have to adjust. Raven is a solid gymnast, particularly on beam, and she's going to be part of our team."

Nadia stiffened. Beam was *her* event. And her pride was still wounded from placing second to an eight-year-old at Regionals.

Judi's cell phone buzzed in her pocket.

"That must be them," she said. "I'd like you all to warm up and stretch each other out while I greet Raven and her mother." With that, Judy strode off toward her glass-enclosed office. Everything at the Bellevue Gymnasium was state-of-the-art and fancy—from the crash mats to the cappuccino machine.

"Raven? What kind of name is that?" Nadia complained. "Are we accepting Disney Channel cast-offs now?"

"Be nice," Jamie chastened.

"You know how much I hate new people," Nadia said.

"I was new!" Jamie said.

"Well, I hated you," said Nadia.

"But now you love me." Jamie smiled as she rested her head on Nadia's shoulder.

"Love is a strong word," Nadia replied.

Jamie was the only one who could lift Nadia's mood. Jamie was competitive without taking anything personally and Nadia respected that.

Jamie remembered her own first day as a Bellevue Kip. From her very first step onto the floor, Jamie could smell success—it was all lemony freshness and high tech heaven.

She and her mom had moved to Seattle from Miami in September to be closer to her grandmother. In a few short months, Jamie had already medaled in three major competitions. Not bad for the new girl.

The squad hopped off the beam and began reluctantly running laps, swaying their arms beside them for momentum as they went. Their gym, like their leotards, was all shiny and decorated in fuchsia, silver, and black.

Kelley jogged ahead. She was happy to have new energy on the squad, but she wasn't sure she was ready to deal with yet another change.

Over the past few months, Kelley had had to cut way back on

soccer and dance in order to compete at the gymnastics level she wanted *and* she'd injured her shoulders. Jamie's grandmother had been hospitalized. Sara, one of their strongest competitors, developed Obsessive Compulsive Disorder from the stress of trying to be perfect in gym and in life. And Bethany, Kelley's former best friend, had grown three inches throwing off her center of gravity and making her impossibly moody. She'd basically pitched a giant temper tantrum at Nationals, decided she and Kelley weren't friends anymore, and switched to rhythmic gymnastics and silks classes.

Things were okay between the girls now, but it wasn't like it used to be. Bethany was still jealous of Kelley's friendship with Jamie, and there didn't seem to be anything Kelley could do to fix things.

As the girls finished their laps, Kelley caught a glimpse of the new girl. She stood beside Judy looking around at the gym as if it were the chewed-up piece of gum stuck to the bottom of her heel. The imitation-daylight overhead lights brought out the subtlest sparkle of gold glitter in her otherwise jet-black hair.

I just hope she fits in, Kelley thought. *The last thing our squad needs is more drama.*

CHAPTER 2: RAVEN

"Oh my god, she looks just like Tyra Banks!" Jamie whispered.

"No, prettier," said Kelley.

"No, shorter," Nadia corrected. "At least we won't have to deal with another gymnast with height issues." They were all a bit scarred by Bethany's drama-filled attempts to prevent a growth spurt.

Raven was about four foot one with a slim but muscular build and skin the deep rich brown of espresso beans. Her hair was pulled back into a bun, the fly-away strands held in place with a simple blue and gold bandana. She wore an electric blue leotard with pale gold tights—definitely not Kip colors.

The girls pretended to stretch on the mats so they could check her out while Judi showed her around.

The whole squad needed extra stretching to prevent injuries now that they were competing at level 8. Kelley had stressed her shoulders and Nadia had to be careful not to twist her ankle again.

"I'm sure she's a good gymnast, too," said Jamie. "She's built for acrobatics."

"We'll see about that," said Nadia.

"Her posture's almost as good as yours, Nadia," said Kelley.

"Almost," said Nadia. Everything about Nadia's tight muscular build was classic gymnast, from her broad shoulders to the short bob of her blond-brown hair.

Nadia was also built for acro.

As if to prove it, Nadia strode over to an empty mat, ran, and launched her lithe body into a Back 1-3/4 with 1/2 Twist, Stretched, which involved changing directions in mid-air and going straight from an aerial twist into a forward roll into a standing position.

It was a level D floor sequence.

Kelley watched poor Raven's facial expression swing from stunned to impressed to confused to slightly irritated.

"Show off much?" Kelley whispered to Jamie.

"She's just marking her territory," said Jamie.

"Yeah," said Kelley. "Like a dog."

"We should say hello." Jamie popped up off the mat and strode over to greet Raven, wearing her biggest, friendliest smile. She remembered how intimidating had been for her to join such a competitive group and she wanted Raven to feel welcomed. Plus, she was excited not to be the newbie anymore.

"Hi, I'm Jamie and this is Kelley," she said. "That's Nadia. She prances like a panther, but she's all puppy dog inside."

"Um, okay," said Raven looking totally confused. She took in everyone's black and fuchsia outfits. "Do I have to wear pink to fit in or is there room for personality in this gym?" she asked.

"Wear what you like," said Kelley.

"Team colors are only required for competition," said Jamie.

"Good to know," said Raven.

"Squad, Raven. Raven, squad," Judi said with forced chipperness. "Now, let's get to it. We have a lot to get done today."

Judi had them all run a circuit of the four women's gymnastics events—beam, uneven bars, floor routine, and vault. Raven didn't say much, but she didn't have to. Her acrobatic and artistic ability spoke for itself.

She was a tumbling powerhouse. Her routine on uneven bars was strong and included a few moves none of the Kips had tried before. Her vault was clean and carried a high degree of difficulty.

When they got to the floor mats, Raven calmly took her place in the corner for her tumbling run. After four long strides, she launched into a Full-in Full out, flipping, tucking and twisting her body. It was a move that required an incredibly strong double layout and tight body positioning. It was level E.

"One level up from Nadia's show-off tumble," Kelley whispered to Jamie. She felt both impressed and nervous at the same time.

With her head high and her facial expression pleased but calm, Raven joined the rest of the group just outside the mat. She didn't look at Nadia and she didn't gloat, but her message was clear. Raven was not going to be intimidated.

"Whoa, nice Full-in, Full-out," said Jamie. She brushed a stray curl off her creamy cocoa forehead. "So why did you change gyms?"

"My parents got a divorce," Raven said, "According to Google Maps, this club is equidistant from their houses. Split down the middle, just like everything else."

"I know how you feel," said Jamie. "I had a hard time leaving my squad in Miami. But the Kips are great, really. And this gym has everything."

"Yeah," said Kelley, "There's even a steam room."

"Are we going to chat all day?" Nadia cut in, "Or are we here to train?"

Nadia's facial expression didn't shift during Raven's tumbling run— she had the world's best poker face—but when it came time to work on beam, Nadia pulled out all the stops. She performed her difficult dismount better than she had done at Regionals and in the two short weeks since she'd been working with Kelley, her artistry had already improved. Raven's beam routine was good, but not Nadia-good. She'd have to step up her degree of difficulty if she wanted to be in contention for a medal in that event.

Vault was where Raven really shone. She had a strong stride and perfect pre-launch positioning. She seemed to know instinctively that the key to getting good height on vault was everything that happened before you were even airborne. Her mid-air twists and somersaults were perfect.

"New Girl 2, Nadia 1," Jamie joked to Kelley, careful not to let Nadia hear. Then out loud she added, "Looks like Raven is going to give us some fierce competition at Nationals."

We'll see about that, Nadia thought as she watched Raven fly over the vault in yet another perfect Yurchenko. *We'll just wait and see.*

CHAPTER 3: QUEEN OF THE GYM

"No, it's like just as competitive as gymnastics, but in a different way. Once you're in, you're in," a familiar girl's voice chattered away as Nadia walked into the locker room the next day.

"There are auditions but no judges and scoring and stuff. They look at you as a performer on the whole—not like how you happened to do in the thirty seconds you were in front of them. It's a whole process." The voice was overly dramatic and the last word of every sentence ended in a kind of croak. Everything about it said, "Obviously, I am superior."

"Bethany," Nadia greeted her former squad-mate. "Kind of you to join us."

Bethany used to be a fulltime Kip, but now only trained with them on Tuesdays and Thursdays. She was visibly taller than she'd been only a few months ago. Her family was supermodel tall and instead of fighting genetics, Bethany had decided to focus on rhythmic and silks training where height wasn't such a disadvantage. Rhythmics was still an Olympic event, but you could also use it to have a much longer career performing in venues like Cirque du Soleil or cruise ships.

"Nadia! Charming as always." Bethany stood to give Nadia double cheek kisses, as if they were European. Then she sat back down on the locker room bench where she'd been holding court with stories of ribbons, hoops, and sparkle sticks. They fake-smiled at one another.

Nadia resented that Bethany had cut back on training. It was like giving up on gymnastics and on the team. Bethany thought Nadia was too harsh.

Bethany wore a new black leotard with a spray of fuchsia like shattered glass across one arm. Her tights shimmered silver and she wore the slenderest of silver headbands to help hold back her thick blond ponytail.

"Back from the cruise-ship circuit so soon?" Nadia half-joked.

Bethany pouted, which only seemed to highlight her pale pink lip gloss.

"Nope, Vegas," Bethany half-joked back.

She's always been more of a performer than a competitor, Nadia thought. Bethany liked the audience, playing to the crowd, the magical this-moment-is-everything-feeling of being in the spotlight. *No wonder she'd quit.*

Nadia felt a sudden pang of jealousy. She scrunched her nose, confused.

"Are we here to work or do each other's make-up?" she snipped as she strode past the rest of the squad toward her locker. She caught a quick glimpse of Raven's blue and gold leotard.

That girl has got to get over her old squad, Nadia thought, irritated. *She's a Kip now.*

Nadia yanked off her scarf and coat and tossed them in her locker. They fell out and she practically growled at them as she stuffed them back inside. She couldn't get them away from her fast enough. It was hot in the locker room and everything that touched her felt suffocating.

There had been a constant pulsing pressure running through her body lately just below her skin. She didn't know if she should go for a run or take a nap. Nothing helped make that tension go away—not tumbling, not sprinting, not screaming at the top of her lungs. Nadia thought maybe punching something might help, but that had never been her style.

"Anyway, you like really get to fly," Nadia heard Bethany say as she pushed open the locker room door and the rest of the girls followed her outside.

She's not even on the team and she can still get the other girls to follow her around like puppy dogs. Even the new girl lets her prattle on without interrupting.

Nadia had liked Bethany. She was competitive. She was good. But Nadia liked it better now that Bethany wasn't around as much.

The gym was no place for drama.

Nadia rubbed her temples, pulled her hair back off her face, and joined her squad out on the mats. She made a mental note to ask Judi for an ibuprofen.

"I don't mean flying like you do on vault or uneven bars," Bethany was saying. "I mean *really* flying. Like on the trapeze."

"Do you get to climb those silk ropes and do flips and twists and stuff at the top?" Jamie asked eagerly.

"Every day," said Bethany. "You can't imagine the adrenaline rush. I'm applying to a circus training camp in Montreal, Canada for the summer. It's really competitive."

"What? So you can be a pole dancer at a club someday?" Nadia took her place on the mats and began her warm-up ritual. "Or maybe a human jump rope?"

Bethany glared at Nadia. Kelley looked awkwardly at Raven as if to apologize.

Everyone feel bad for the new girl, Nadia thought. *How tedious.*

Nadia's head pounded. And she felt tired—again.

It didn't help that Bethany wouldn't stop talking about the circus.

Circus Camp! "A serious dedicated gymnast wants to be a human jump rope," Nadia muttered to herself."

"I'm actually too short to be the human jump rope," Bethany said with a wink. "But I can work my way up to it if I grow."

"I'm glad to see your sense of humor has returned," Nadia said.

"Looks like you've taken over for me."

"I'm too tired to bicker," Nadia said, lengthening into a side bend.

"Maybe it's a growth spurt," Bethany said pointedly.

"That would be remarkable," said Nadia. "My mother's 5 3' and my father's a whopping 5'6". I don't think there are any growth spurts in my near future, but if you have a crystal ball, I'm happy to look."

"Hey!" Jamie said, swiftly shifting the conversation. "Raj Bhansar performs for Cirque du Soleil now! The Olympic silver medalist from 2008? It's like a really big deal. I saw online that there are 50 former Olympians performing for Cirque."

"Do you guys wonder about that?" Raven asked. She adjusted her headband and twisted into a glute stretch. "What you'll do when you're too old for gym?"

"All the time!" Jamie exclaimed.

"Paul Bowler is coaching," Kelley added.

"Yeah, and lots of gymnasts go into broadcasting, sport medicine, or sports psychology," said Jamie. "There are lots of options."

"Shawn Johnson came in second on *Dancing with the Stars*," Bethany added.

Nadia grimaced. "That's a good thing?"

She took deep cleansing breaths, but it was hard to concentrate with the other girls buzzing in her ears like annoying flies.

Coaching was clearly the only respectable option for a former-gymnast. Her mother had taught her to "go out on top." You retire after you win Olympic gold, then you quietly disappear for a while until you make your grand re-entry as the coach of Olympic Gold. That was the kind of career Nadia wanted. The only career there was.

"The point is, it's not like your life is over once you can't compete anymore," Jamie said.

"Only the best part," Nadia grumped.

Clap clap clap.

Clap clap clap.

Judi called the squad to order.

"Okay, ladies, we have a lot to get done today. We're going to focus on basic conditioning, strengthening, and stretching, including a segment designed to help us build artistry into dance series for floor routines," Judi announced.

Nadia didn't make a facial expression, but on the inside she was groaning.

Of course, as if this day hasn't gotten off to a bad enough start already. She shook out her shoulders, already uncomfortable.

She felt like going home, hiding under her comforter and watching a movie about gymnastics instead of training for it. It wasn't like her.

"We'll start small and build up today," Judi said. "First, general conditioning and tumbling. We're going to work a lot of double fronts into the pit and then build up to an Arabian Double Front. Jamie, what's an Arabian Double Front?"

"It's a 1/2 twist into front somersault done with two front somersaults, instead of just one."

You can do it in pike, tuck, open or layout," added Kelley.

"Good," said Judy.

Too easy, Nadia thought. Judi sometimes went on a kick about reinforcing basics. The pit was a giant pit of foamy bits, kind of like the ball bin at Chuck E. Cheese.

"Nadia, please begin."

Nadia ran, jumped onto a springboard, and did two forward rolls in the air. She didn't get enough height to complete the rotations and landed on her butt in the crush pit.

Scowling, she climbed her way out.

"Thank you, Nadia," said Judi. "Squad, as you can see, building enough height and rotation for this skill is difficult. The setup is extremely important. We are going to work a LOT of double fronts into the crash pit today until you get enough of a feel for this skill to move on. Raven, you're up."

Raven took a deep breath and moved to the head of the crash mat. She ran, sprang and completed two perfect somersaults in the air landing on her feet in the crash pit.

Judi clapped. "Nicely done. Nadia, did you see that she was careful not to overextend her legs on the landing? That saves your knees. Bethany, you're up next."

Bethany approached the somersaults with confidence and skill. She was calm and unstressed.

It made Nadia angry.

The squad worked the double fronts over and over again until they had all perfected the landing and could do the move without even thinking about it.

Nadia didn't land on her butt again, but she felt off all afternoon.

Once they had progressed into a Double Arabian front in the crash pit and then could do it on floor, Judi announced that it was time to work on dance.

"Max will be here later this week to work with you on specific choreography for your floor routines, but in the meantime, I want us all improving on basics."

Jamie leaned over to Raven. Max is our choreographer. You're going to love him. He's awesome.

Raven half-smiled, unsure.

"Kelley is going to lead you all through some ballet-inspired strength and stretch while I shut things down in my office. I have to leave on time today. Good work on your tumbles, girls."

With that, Judi headed for her office, already pulling her curly red hair out of its braid.

Kelley bounced to the front of the mat. She'd been studying dance since she was three years old. Her mom had later enrolled her in gymnastics when her dance teacher said that Kelley kept tumbling every time she stepped on the mat.

Is it really necessary to be that chipper? Nadia thought.

"Okay," said Kelley, way too excited for Nadia's mood. "As you know, dance elements are an opportunity to connect with the music and the audience."

"Yeah," agree Jamie. "Empty pauses between tumbling routines are so dull."

"And ballet moves like relevés and retirés are really good ways to build up strength in all the balancing muscles in your ankles." Kelley demonstrated by connecting her feet at the heels, and rising slowly up onto her toes as she lifted her arms above her head.

"Ugh," said Nadia, already bored. "Everyone knows artistry doesn't count nearly as much as acro anymore. Every second on that mat is a chance to earn another tenth of a point and you don't do that with a reliver."

"It's relevé," said Bethany.

"Whatever."

"She's just crabby 'cause she can't do it," Bethany told Raven.

"I have no problem with artistry," said Nadia, her voice strong but cold.

"Then why did you come in second all-around when your acro is so strong? Don't you think it's cause you have the grace of a hippo?"

"Why did you come in tenth?" Nadia shot back. "Don't you think it's cause you crashed into the vault?"

Bethany took a step toward Nadia and Jamie quickly moved between them.

Nadia and Bethany stood staring at each other, nostrils flaring.

"You're both insane," Raven said.

"Raven's right, guys," said Jamie. "You need to chill. Every gymnast should have some degree of grace."

Nadia moved to another mat, put her headset on and focused on working her oversplits while everyone else continued with their ballet stretches.

Children, Nadia thought as she stretched her legs wide. An oversplit was like a regular split with even more extension. The angle between your legs went beyond 180 degrees.

"She's just showing off again," said Bethany. "She has to make sure everyone knows she's queen of the gym."

They thought Nadia couldn't hear them talking about her because she had her earbuds in, but she heard every word.

Nadia shot them a death glare.

Typical, she thought. *They're always excluding me. Always making me the bad guy.*

"Leave her alone." Jamie scolded. "Nadia has a hard shell," she explained to Raven, "but she also has a soft underbelly. She's really warm and kindhearted once you get to know her."

She's apologizing for my personality, Nadia thought. *Nice.* Tears welled up in her eyes. Nadia was startled. It was not like her to cry. She quickly blinked them away.

"I can hear you," she said in her slowest, coldest, most precise voice.

Bethany's face flushed a bright pink, but she quickly covered for herself.

"Well, it's true," she said, pushing her shoulders back and pulling her head higher. "You'll never win gold if you keep holding your arms like that. Who cares if you have good extension if you look like a clod."

Nadia's nostrils flared, but she didn't say anything. She didn't trust her own voice not to give out. She tried to make her face look steely and cold. Then she walked slowly toward the locker room without looking back. Halfway there, the tears started streaming down her cheeks.

She didn't understand why everything they said made her feel so bad. It's not like they'd never excluded her before. But today she felt totally alone—like her whole squad didn't get her. Didn't even like her.

It hurt—bad.

Never let them see you cry, she thought.

Not even when your heart is breaking.

* * * * * * * * * * * * * * * * * * *

Raven waved good-bye to the rest of the squad and headed outside to wait for her dad. She sighed, tired and worn-out from the day's workout and intro to team drama. She couldn't stand fighting.

She silently watched the rest of the squad get into mini-vans and sport utility vehicles and drive away. *There's a lot of girlie-drama to get used to on this squad,* she thought. *There always is.*

The problem was Raven was already tired. Tired of adjusting to new situations. And tired of other people's issues.

"Hey, you seem a little overwhelmed." Jamie walked up beside Raven and put a friendly hand on her shoulder. "It gets easier," she said. "Everyone's really cool once you get to know them. Today was kind of an off day. I remember when I first started I—"

A car horn honked.

"Just takes time, right?" said Raven.

"Yep," Jamie smiled as a beat-up brown hatchback pulled up in front of them. "And don't worry about Nadia. It's not personal. She's just, well, Nadia."

"I guess," Raven shrugged.

"You need a ride?" Jamie asked.

"No, thanks," Raven said as Jamie pulled open the rusty old car door. The woman in the driver's seat waved excitedly at them. "My dad's on his way."

Or at least he should be, she thought. The new divvied up schedule was hard on everyone. Her dad never seemed to remember which days were his. Then again, that had always sort of been the problem.

Raven shivered as a light mist started falling. Typical Seattle. She went inside and plopped down on the bench outside Judi's office.

"Raven, are your parents on their way?" Judi asked. "I need to lock up."

Raven checked her cell. Twenty-minutes late.

"I think so," said Raven.

Ten-minutes later, Judi had shut down her computer and turned off all the gym lights. Her make-up was done, her hair in an upsweep, her coat was on, and she was checking the wall clock every fifteen seconds.

Raven looked at her guiltily. She could do without the pressure.

"Raven, if your parents are having difficulties picking you up on time, I'm sure you could get a ride with one of the others."

"They're on their way," Raven cut her off.

As if this were my fault.

The door whipped open bringing with it a blast of cold damp air. A tall, well-dressed man in a fitted black overcoat and polished shoes rushed straight over to Judi, bypassing Raven. He held out his hand to shake hers.

"Myles Busi. Nice to meet you," he said, quickly taking in Judi's hair and make-up. "I apologize for keeping you from your plans."

"Judi," she blushed, highlighting the spray of freckles on her cheeks and neck.

Raven's dad sometimes had that effect on people.

Raven scowled. She felt the heat of all her anger in her cheeks.

"Well, you look like you have better places to be," he said smiling. "Come on, Raven hurry along."

"I was ready half an hour ago!" Raven huffed as she gathered up her gym bag.

Her dad apologized again to Judi and they were out the door. "I'm sorry, he said. I miscalculated. It's a really long ride." Then turning to Raven, he joked, "You'd better win some medals at Nationals to make all of this worth it!"

Raven's heart sank and another flash of anger overwhelmed her. *She* hadn't wanted to change gyms. Or houses. Or their entire family life. She stomped out the door before he could see her tears.

The rain had picked up and cold icy drops stung her cheeks.

17

Of course he didn't bring me an umbrella, she thought. *I only texted him about it an hour ago!*

She heard the gym door swing open and shut behind her. Her dad's dress shoes echoed on the concrete.

Make it worthwhile, Raven thought bitterly. *For who? For him? As if there isn't enough pressure in gymnastics already.*

As if you ever thought about me.

The tears fell freely now. She wiped at them impatiently.

As if—you even loved me.

CHAPTER 4: DISORDERLY CONDUCT

Kelley balanced on the edge of the beam practicing different basic dismounts, from tucks to pikes. Judi was continuing her back-to-basics workouts this week.

Keeping her feet together, Kelley jumped up off the beam bringing her knees close to her chest in the air and then bent her knees as her feet hit the mat to soften her landing. She lifted her arms above her head and saw Nadia running to the bathroom—again. She'd been doing that a lot today.

Kelley felt bad about all the arguing yesterday. Bethany had been hard on Nadia, but Nadia was acting even more snippy than usual. Kelley was glad Bethany wasn't training with them today.

Kelley got back up on the bar and tried a pike dismount. She brought her legs up to a horizontal in the air before landing.

Raven walked over with Jamie and stood beside the beam.

"Do you think she's puking?" Raven asked.

"What? At my performance?" joked Kelley. "It wasn't that bad." Kelley brushed a straggly strand of brown hair away from her face.

"No, like bulimia," Raven clarified.

"Nadia keeps running to the bathroom," Jamie explained.

"Well, we're not eating anything during practice so that can't be it," Kelley said. "There's nothing to throw up unless she's sneaking granola bars from the vending machine."

"Maybe she's obsessively washing her hands like Sara?" Jamie suggested. Their former squad-mate had washed her hands over and over again to soothe herself when the pressure to win had gotten too intense. It was only one of many repetitive rituals she'd picked up over time and the girls still felt bad for not noticing sooner.

"It's not like Nadia to copy someone else's disorder," Kelley pointed out. "She'd have to get one of her own that was even worse."

Jamie slapped her gently on the arm, but she was stifling a laugh.

"This is serious."

"I know," said Kelley, "But what could it be?"

"Maybe she has food poisoning," Raven suggested.

"And she refuses to miss training for even one day?" Jamie joked. "I think you hit it.

"I'll go check on her," Kelley offered. "I got food poisoning last year from bad fish. Not fun. She probably needs a ginger ale or something."

Kelley headed to the locker room and slowly opened the door. A quiet feeling of dread welled up in her stomach and chest. She wasn't sure what she was about to find and she wasn't sure why that scared her.

"Nadia?" she called softly. "Nad?"

Kelley heard a muffled sound in the back by the bathroom stalls and followed it.

A mass shifted slightly beneath one of the stalls and Kelley stopped dead.

A sudden feeling of dread gripped her chest like a big boney hand grabbing her heart.

Nadia was balled up on the bathroom floor, her face resting on her arms.

"Nadia, are you crying?" Kelley asked gently. Kelley had been around a lot of crying friends. Bethany cried just about every other day. But Nadia never cried. Hearing her sniffle now frightened Kelley.

Nadia didn't answer.

"Let me in?" Kelley asked gently.

Nadia's shoulders gently shook up and down.

Kelley slowly pushed open the stall door and squatted down beside her friend.

Nadia had bunched her lean body up into a heap on the floor. Her shoulders shook. A maxi pad wrapper was strewn on the floor beside her alongside an un-used tampon.

"Oh!" Kelley exclaimed, standing up again.

Kelley caught a glimpse of red in the toilet.

Nadia had gotten her period.

Kelley reached beyond Nadia and flushed. She didn't need the visuals.

Her own hand shook. She hadn't gotten her period yet—gymnasts were usually late-bloomers—and she didn't want it.

"I'm sorry," she said, near panic.

"I can't I can't—" Nadia heaved between sobs. "I can't use the tampon. I just can't."

Nadia crossed her arms over her stomach and bent forward.

"It hurts so much. I can't move."

"You don't have to," soothed Kelley. She awkwardly leaned over and brushed a strand of Nadia's chestnut brown hair away from her eyes.

"We're gymnasts!" Nadia finally cried between sobs. "We're all muscle. We aren't supposed to get our periods until later. My mom didn't get hers until she was fifteen! Some don't even get their periods until they're twenty. Why am I getting it now? Am I not strong enough? I thought. I thought I was an acrobat –I thought."

"Is this the first time?" Kelley asked.

Nadia nodded.

"It hurts so badly. I can't move." She looked up at Nadia. "And it's so gross. It's not just blood. It's—"

That was enough. Kelley shot to her feet and bolted like a deer startled by a random sound.

"I'm going to go get Judi," she said.

Kelley ran to her coach, heart pounding. She heard Nadia's sobs grow louder as the locker room door swung wide behind her.

She nestled up next to Jamie on the mat, watching Judi carefully enter the locker room.

"What happened?" Raven asked, her eyes wide.

Kelley's hands were still shaking.

"Nadia got her period," Kelley announced.

"Oh my god!" Jamie squealed. "But leotards are so revealing, how do you even where a pad?"

"You can't, right?" said Raven. "I mean right?"

"Male gymnasts have it so easy," Kelley said. "They hit puberty and they just get stronger leaner muscles. That's so awesome for gymnastics."

"I know!" said Jamie. "And we just get cramps and—" Jamie paused. "Do you think she'll still be able to compete?"

"Of course, she will!" said Raven. "It's not a disease."

"I know!" said Jamie, "but it can be so…intense. I heard about this one girl in Miami who bled right through her leotard. She had to perform her entire beam routine with all the judges looking at her and her—"

Just then, Nadia's mom walked calmly through the front door and into the locker room, focused, as if it were the finish line. Nadia's mom had also been a really well-known gymnast in Canada.

A few minutes later, Nadia walked out wrapped up in her winter gear and crumpled up against her mother.

Kelley shivered. "I hate to say this, but I'm *so* glad it's not me."

"Me, too," said Raven.

"Me, three," said Jamie.

CHAPTER 5: GRUMP FOR A DAY

Raven ran on tiptoes toward the locker room and glanced at the clock.

Twenty-minutes late.

Jees, dad, she thought as she dumped her bag on the bench, yanked off her sweatpants, and re-adjusted her brown and turquoise leotard. *You didn't even have to pick me up. You just had to get out the door on time.*

Raven was fuming. She'd taken the bus to his house from school. All he'd had to do was be there to drive her to practice.

Couldn't even do that.

Jamie and Kelley were already gathered on the mats where Judi was prepping them for today's practice. That meant they'd already run laps and they'd already stretched. *Where was everyone else?* Raven hoped someone was running even later than her.

"Nationals are coming up in a few short months," said Judi. "This is big."

With her head down, Raven quietly slunk toward the mats and sat down next to Jamie.

Maybe Judi won't—

"Raven," Judi said sternly, glaring at her. "You get to be late *once* on this team. Your free pass is used up. On time and ready to work. Tell your parents."

Like it would do any good, Raven thought.

From across the mat, Kelley mouthed, "Don't worry. I'm always late," but it didn't make Raven feel any better. *She'd* been on time. *She'd*

23

been ready to work. It was her stupid father who couldn't get it together—

"Kelley, that will be enough," Judi snapped. "Raven, the rest of the squad is already warmed up, "Go run five laps and stretch out," Judi said. "Then meet us at the vault. And do *not* rush your stretches."

Raven's cheeks burned. She liked being the center of attention, but only when it was for something good. People glaring and yelling at her just made her want to sink into the floor and down a rabbit hole.

Jamie gently nudged her and Raven got to her feet and took off running.

Anything to get away from the death glare, she thought. *It's like they name someone to be Grump for the day at every practice.*

Raven's anger grew bigger with every step. She wanted to hit something and right now, that something was her parents.

"Watch your form, Raven!" Judi called. "We don't skimp in this gym. Not even in warm-ups."

I'd hit Judi, too, Raven thought. Her old coach never yelled at her. Her old coach was chill. Her old coach would have understood.

Raven's feet pounded against the gym floor.

Why couldn't they just stay together so I could have one *life with* one *house and* one *gym? Why even have a kid if you're going to move far apart and make her shuttle back and forth? You can't call halfsies on someone else's life.*

As she passed the vault, she saw Jamie perform an effortless Yurchenko, with a twist entry into a piked back flip. Raven ran faster. Jamie was cool enough, but this whole squad bickered too much. Raven missed her team. She missed her friends. She spent so much time in transit, it was like she never got to see them at all.

At least I go to private school, Raven thought, *or I'd have to change that too!*

She tried to calm herself down by taking deep cleansing breaths before stretching. She tried to focus on her breath and push all the anger away, picturing the inside of her head as a blue sky. The anger was storm clouds. The sun wanted to come out. It was time for the clouds to float away.

The clouds were stubborn.

By the time Raven joined Jamie and Kelley on vault, she felt a little calmer—or at least ready to work. Vault was one of her favorites. It was impossible to think about anything else during a vault. There was no room for mistakes—not even tiny ones. You had to be 100% focused.

Too bad it only lasted seven seconds.

Vault and floor were the only two gymnastics events that both men and women performed. Raven's old gym was co-ed. She'd liked showing off her strength to her guy friends. She'd liked being better than them.

"We all did Yurchenko-style vaults with a round-off entry for state finals," Jamie explained. "And Tsukaharas with a quarter turn in pre-flight for Regionals."

Raven nodded. "I can do those. No problem."

The vaulting table was 4 feet 3 inches high. Vaults were kind of like the houses in Harry Potter. There were five different groups or families, based on the way they started. And they were all named after the gymnast who first performed them. The most popular were the Yurchenko, the Tsukahara and the front handspring style.

Raven loved that there was room for innovation in gymnastics—that all the moves they were doing right now on vault were invented or at least first performed by someone her own age as recently as the 1980s.

In the highest levels of competitions, like US National Championships, gymnasts performed one vault in team and individual all-around events, and two vaults from different families in the individual vault finals and to qualify for the event finals.

"We can perform any vault we want for Nationals, right?" Raven asked.

"As long as it's difficult," Kelley winked. Most gymnasts went the vault with the highest start value they could perform without messing up for competition. No one was going for the silver. They all wanted gold.

"Of course it's going to be difficult," Raven said, a little too snippy. *Okay, so maybe the meditation hadn't worked.*

Raven still had some anger left in her as she got into position at the start of the runway. She stared down the vault imagining it was her parents. She told herself that if she made it over, if she twisted just right, she could turn back time and glue her family back together.

Raven took a deep breath and did a round-off onto the springboard followed by a twist entry into a piked back flip. Pushing off the vault, she launched herself into the air for a full twist followed by two back flips. It was a kind of Yurchenko vault named after Russian gymnast, Svetlana Khorkina.

"Whoa," exclaimed Jamie. "Your vaults—it's like you're being shot out of a rocket."

Raven smiled. "Thank you...I—"

"Yes," Judi interrupted. "All force and no flair. I want you to try again, and this time, add a little grace.

Raven's cheeks flushed. For a brief second she felt like hiding.

If Judi wants to be crabby, that's her problem, she thought. *My vaults I can fix.*

Raven moved to the start of the runway, took four long strides, did a kind of cartwheel, hit the springboard and twisted her body in the air so that she was facing the other way by the time her hands touched in the vault for the push-off. Then twisting in the air, she brought her legs up horizontal to the ground and flipped backwards twice before landing facing the mat.

She stuck her landing without a wobble. She smiled.

"Rocket," said Judi. "Try again."

Raven felt like she'd been slapped. She gaped at Kelley, wide-eyed. Kelly just shrugged.

Why is she being so hard on me today? Raven thought.

"Better yet," Judi said, "Watch Jamie,"

"I'm sorry," Jamie mouthed as she moved to the runway, but her eyes looked proud.

"Jamie's had a hard time with vault," Kelley explained. "It took her forever to learn the Tsuk, but now she does it great every time." Kelley pointed her left toe out in front of her and moved her foot around in a circle.

Jamie performed the same vault. It was beautiful. But Raven couldn't see how it was that much different than her own.

She just didn't get it.

What does she want from me? she thought. *At least that grumpy girl hasn't shown up yet.*

Kelley was up next. Her body was out of position on the tuck, which led to a wobble on her landing. She clutched her ankle.

"Are you okay?" Judi asked.

"Yes," said Kelley a little too quickly. "I just need to walk it off." Kelley walked gingerly off the mat.

Jamie moved to her as Raven headed for the runway and took the vault again from the top. This time, she focused on the strength in her arms, the tightness of her stomach muscles as she turned in the air. She imagined elongating her legs. She imagined herself in a tutu.

"No, Raven. Again."

Tired and frustrated, Raven tried again. This time, her vault was faster than the last. She was angry. She wanted to fly. She wanted to get away.

"That's enough for today, Raven," Judi said. "But I want you to practice some of the ballet moves at home that Kelley taught you yesterday. You have to be more patient on the vault. The goal is not to get it over with as quickly as possible."

"Sure thing, coach," Raven grumbled. Then, under her breath, she added, "Maybe Judi has her period, too."

"Raven, that will be enough," said Judi. "I am hard on you because I want you to improve. When we start blaming all female moods on our periods, we do a disservice to women."

Raven sat down to stretch while Jamie performed another perfect vault and left the mat glowing.

Kelley took two steps into her run and stopped.

"It feels wobbly," she said.

"Your ankle? Judi asked.

Kelley nodded.

"Consider yourself benched," Judi said. "I want you to rest, ice, compress, and elevate that foot. Twenty minutes on. Twenty minutes off with the ice pack all night. We'll re-evaluate tomorrow."

"But I need to train. Nationals are only—"

"You need to heal."

* * * * * * * * * * * * * * * * * *

Kelley tried to walk toward her mom's minivan with even strides. Her mom was iffy enough on the time required for gymnastics. She didn't need to see Kelley injured, too.

She put on her biggest fake smile as she opened the car door. The rich smells of warm chicken soon filled the car. A silver and fuchsia thermos sat on the front seat.

"Mmmm," she said. "Smells like soup."

"I brought you a thermos," her mom said. "And there's a fresh bottle of water in the backseat if you want it."

"Thanks!" said Kelley, diving right in.

"There's real dinner waiting for you at home, but I know how hungry you are after practice. I thought you should get some nourishment in you right away."

"You're the best!" Kelley exclaimed.

"I try," said her mom, watching Kelley carefully. She was already suspicious.

Kelley sat her butt down on the front seat and then gently pivoted, bringing her legs in behind her. She'd finished out the rest of practice with her foot up and iced, watching Jamie and Raven get extra training on vault.

Nadia never showed.

Periods must be awful, she thought as a feeling of distant dread crept up on her.

Kelley shivered involuntarily.

Mistake. Kelley's mom's hand was on her forehead in a heartbeat.

"Do you feel okay?" she asked. "Do you have a fever?"

"No. I was just—"

"What's wrong with your ankle?"

Kelley pulled the car door shut behind her. *She sees everything!*

"I just tweaked it a little. It's fine."

"You don't look fine. You look like you're in pain. And I do not like the way you just hobbled across the parking lot."

"I didn't hobble," Kelley said, but her voice was tired and she didn't want to argue.

"I don't know what we're going to do, Kelley. First your shoulder,

28

now your ankle."

"It happens, mom, Kelley shrugged. It's part of being an athlete."

Kelley's mom scrunched her eyebrows as she pulled out of the parking lot.

"I wish you would just stick to soccer! There are far fewer injuries."

"Are you kidding me?" Kelley sat up in her seat. "Katie has broken her collarbone twice over the past three years. Julie fractured her elbow. Maria tore the tendon in her finger when the ball slammed her on a corner kick. Her fingertip still dangles a little like a witch." Kelley's voice got more and more animated a she spoke. "Mai sprained both her ankles. Alyx chipped a tooth. When Edie went up for a header last week, she whacked the back of the other girl's head instead of the ball and had a goose egg the size of a tennis ball on her head for a week. It turned into two black eyes and the principal called her parents in for a conference cause she thought someone had hit her."

"And that's just my team! The pros get injured all the time. Remember when we were watching the Olympics and—"

Kelley noticed her mom's eyes widen. She looked like she might vomit.

"I'm not helping myself here, am I?"

"Not much, no."

Kelley's mind scrambled for a few seconds. Then she smiled.

"Well, if you want, I can always sit in front of the TV every night and play video games."

"That sounds safe. I'd like that."

"Yep," said Kelley. "Then maybe I'll get really obese and die of heart disease or type two diabetes or—"

"No thank you."

Kelley laughed. "I wish I'd known that's what it took to win my argument. I've been stressing for so long! Glad I've finally won you over."

"I'll tell you what?" said her mom as they turned into their driveway. "You can play all the sports you like, just as long as you wear a helmet, a mouth guard, and bubble wrap."

"I'll definitely win gold in those," said Kelley.

Her mom turned the key shutting down the engine. She looked at

Kelley and held her fist out for a pound.

"Deal?"

"You're kind of a dork, mom." Kelley's fist met her mother's.

"But I love you!"

CHAPTER 6: BRUISED AND BUMMED OUT

"Oh my god, I'm SO sore!" Jamie exclaimed as she plopped down on the mat beside Kelley, Raven, and Bethany. They'd already run their laps and were stretching out before the day's work out. Yesterday's tumbling drills had been tough. Kelley taped up her ankle while Bethany chatted with Raven about her silks class.

"I love your bandana," she said. "It's so…Sometimes this squad can be so strict about their dress code."

"You started the dress code!" cried Kelley. She tossed her tape roll at Bethany's head. Bethany ducked and it rolled across the floor.

Bethany shrugged. "No Nadia?"

"She has her period," Raven said, lowering her voice on the last word."

"Thank God there was a reason for all that moody!" said Bethany. "She was cranky even by Nadia standards"

Poor Nadia, Jamie thought. *I bet she hasn't missed this much training since she had the chicken pox. She must be dying.* Jamie cringed. She thought about all the days her grandma had been cooped up in the hospital around Thanksgiving. She silently counted her blessings. She felt bad for Nadia, but her period would pass. And Jamie was glad her grandma was strong and healthy again. No more hospital.

Jamie's eyes rested on Kelley's ankle.

"Does Judi know it's purple?" she asked.

"She saw it when it was green." Kelley joked, but Jamie could tell she was still worried.

"Well, I think it's a lovely color," Bethany said. "You should get a leotard to match. It brings out the gold flecks in your eyes."

Kelley made a face and Raven laughed.

"I have a bandana that would totally go with that bruise," she teased.

Raven looked up as Judi walked over and joined the squad on the mat. Her unruly red curls were held back by an assortment of butterfly clips and she wore one of Jamie's favorite coach-Judi fuchsia and silver jumpsuits.

Judi crossed her legs and the squad formed a circle around her, exchanging worried glances. Judi never sat with them—not even when she had explained about Sara's OCD.

"I get the sense you are all a bit weirded out by Nadia's absence," she began.

"It's been like three days!" Jamie exclaimed, horrified. "Are periods really that bad?"

"She's like the toughest Kip," Kelley noted. "If a period could knock her out, what would it do to the rest of us?"

Raven sat quietly, scrutinizing Judi's face.

The hint of a smile played at the corners of Judi's mouth. "Sometimes, when a girl first gets her period, she just wants to crawl under a pile of blankets and snuggle."

Raven, Jamie, Kelley, and Bethany exchanged a look that clearly said, "I'm glad it's not me."

"Sometimes I want to do that, and I don't even have my period," said Jamie.

Judi smiled. "Me, too. Do you girls have any questions about it?"

"About our periods?" asked Bethany. "No. My mom already gave me that talk."

"Is Nadia going to be okay?" Kelley asked.

"She's going to be just fine and as strong as ever," Judi said. "She just needs to rest for a couple of days. When you first get your period, it can be a little—unpredictable. One month heavy. One month, light. Later, it evens out. Nadia will get used to it and she'll feel better than ever."

"And be back to her old sweet self," said Bethany.

Kelley didn't look convinced.

"It's all very natural," Judi said, "and most of you won't have to deal with it for a while. Now—" She clapped her hands together and stood up. The girls all reluctantly got to their feet and adjusted their leotards.

"Today, we work bars," Judi announced. "Kelley, how's the ankle?"

"Taped, iced, and ready to go," said Kelley.

"Good. Bars are just the thing. We'll give you one more day to heal before the hard tumbling continues and I'll help you down instead of having you dismount. Stick around after practice and we'll massage that ankle." She turned to the rest of the squad.

"I want to start by working the basics and reviewing all the compulsory components for Nationals. Get your hands chalked up and let's get to it."

Judi's energy was contagious. All the girls bounced up off the mats and practically skipped to the uneven bars. Kelley walked slowly and carefully behind them. Her ankle felt better today, but it was still a little swollen and weak. She thought it might actually be a sprain, but she didn't want Judi to think she couldn't work out.

Jamie and Kelley strapped on their grips to support their wrists and protect their palms from the tearing that the friction of spinning around the bars could sometimes cause. Raven and Bethany used chalk instead—to prevent sweaty sticky palms.

Judi handed Jamie an official printout listing all the requirements for Nationals.

"Jamie, please read the requirements for bars."

Jamie walked forward and cleared her throat. "There are a lot of them."

She read out the compulsory components including speed and size of moves, the number of changes from one bar to another, the ways a gymnast had to grip or hold the bars, and changes in direction.

Each routine had to include a release move like a counter swing to handstand or an overshoot with no feet touching the mat and a kip out without bent arms. The dismount had to be least a "B" level, like a layout full twist.

Jamie's heart grew lighter with every word.

"Hey, we already to all of this stuff!" Jamie exclaimed. "Two clear hip circles in a row, a back giant to half-turn…"

I have trained you well," Judi joked. "But as you know, excellent execution is key. Straight arms and body throughout your casts; no laboring or struggling on any of your handstands." She gave Bethany a look. "To that end, we are going to have a little friendly competition." Judi reached mysteriously into the pocket of her track top and pulled out a gift card. "The gymnast with the best form today, gets this gift card to the Sports Silo." She paused for drama. "And I'm not telling you how much it's for."

"Too bad Nadia's not here, she'd love this," Jamie said.

"I'm so winning this," said Bethany.

"Oh, we'll see about that," Kelley joked.

"What do you say we add an extra something to the competition?" Raven said, a mischievous glint in her eye.

"You mean like a bet?" Kelley asked.

"Yes, like a bet. Winner gets the gift card, but worst performance has to do a lip sync with dance moves to "Gangham Style" in front of all the other squads at Nationals.

"No way!" shouted Kelly, already embarrassed. She loved dancing at recitals but she hated showing off in front of other people.

Raven shrugged. "If you don't want to do it, then win."

Jamie's eyes twinkled. Competition made her better. And now she really wanted to win.

"You're on!" she said.

"I'm in," said Bethany.

"Of course you're in! " Kelley joked. "You love being a diva!"

Bethany shrugged. "If you've got it, flaunt it." She and Jamie looked at Kelley expectantly.

"Fine, I'm in too," Kelley said. The four girls sealed the deal with handshakes.

Judi cleared her throat, bringing their attention back to the bars. "As a reminder, ladies, you want to strive to do more than just the minimum requirements. I expect all of you to pull out the best performances of your careers. I need you to be constantly aware of your body positioning. I'm going to post a copy of the official guidelines will all of the compulsory moves for each event on the bulletin board outside my office door. It includes a list of all the deductions and everything you can get extra points for. Read it. Study it. Know it. Got it?"

"Got it," said the squad in unison.

"Now, I have lists of notes for improvement based on your performances at Regionals." Judi held up her clipboard. Neat notes were dashed out in an organizational system only Judi could understand.

"Raven, I have a basic skeleton of your routine from your former coach, but I'll need to see you run through it again so I'll know where to focus our efforts. Then we'll all work on improving our core moves. That's the theme this week, ladies, building blocks."

Raven nodded.

"This should be good," Bethany muttered to Kelley. Kelley shifted awkwardly.

"Way to put the new girl on the spot, Judi," Bethany called out.

"You all have to learn to perform under pressure," Judi said. "Better to start now. Raven, you're up."

Raven ran some extra chalk over her hands and walked toward the uneven bars. If she was nervous, Jamie couldn't tell. Raven didn't look like she was out to impress anyone.

Jamie remembered the first time she had to perform in front of her whole squad. It was also her very first day of practice.

It would have been so hard to fit in if I'd messed up, she thought.

Raven's routine began strong.

She was aggressive and ran through all the compulsory moves and bar changes with seemingly no effort whatsoever.

"Looks like the new girl wants that gift card," Bethany teased, but her lips were tight, her competitive spirit already riled up.

"We can take her," Jamie said.

Raven's routine was solid, gold medal solid, but it wasn't until her dismount that the entire squad started to worry. It was unlike any dismount Jamie had ever seen before.

Starting from a kip—which was basically holding yourself up on the bar with the strength of your outstretched arms—she began to rotate downwards and backwards, leaning her hips against the high bar. Then she let her arms go and rotated around it.

Using the momentum from her hip swing, she flew out and away from the high bar. Quickly, she did a half turn so she was facing the bar and transitioned into two forward rolls mid-air, eventually landing with her feet together, knees bent to absorb the impact.

It was breathtaking.

Jamie jumped up and down and started clapping. "What was that, like a Hip Circle Hecht with—?"

"I don't know, it happened so fast," Kelley said.

"Whatever it was, she dismounted off the high bar," Bethany noted.

"Whoa," said Jamie. "I've never seen anyone do that in competition before."

"I think it's like way advanced," said Bethany.

"More advanced than anything we've ever done," said Kelley.

"More advanced than anything even Nadia has ever done," Jamie said.

"We do stuff like that all the time in aerial training," Bethany said, but her voice sounded shaky. "It's easier than it looks."

Jamie had the flash of an idea. Raven had just upped the ante. They'd all need special dismounts if they hoped to be competitive at Nationals.

"Judi, can we try that dismount?" asked Jamie.

"No," said Judi without explanation.

"But—"

"Discussion closed. We have a full training schedule today. I want to see you all on beam in five minutes."

Jamie watched as her friends walked toward the beam without arguing.

Why does Raven get a special dismount and the rest of us don't? she thought.

She felt the pang of something like jealousy. Except that Jamie never got jealous—except for that one time in Miami when her friend Alex got a super-cool shiny blue leotard that Jamie could never afford in a million years. But she'd gotten over that pretty quickly. Alex gave her all her hand-me-downs anyway.

This felt different. This was already affecting her routine. This affected her dreams. Jamie would have to do some research. She would convince Judi to let her try her own special move. And she would perfect it before Nationals.

Because without a truly spectacular dismount, there was no way she was bringing home gold.

CHAPTER 7: JEALOUS MUCH?

"Hope you've got that lip sync ready, Jamie," Raven teased the next day.

"Double or nothing?" Jamie asked.

"What do you mean, like if you don't do better than me today, I have to like add flips to my lip sync?"

"Yes," said Jamie. It annoyed her that she was feeling so competitive with Raven, but it was what it was.

"Deal." Raven and Jamie fist-pumped, just as the locker room door swung open and shut.

"Nadia!" Jamie ran over and wrapped her arms around Nadia's neck.

The squad gathered around her as if she were a celebrity with a terminal disease.

"What was it like?" Jamie asked. "Did you throw up? My cousin threw up."

"Does your dad know?" asked Raven.

"Did you have to like buy all new underwear?" asked Kelley.

Nadia gave Kelley a pointed stare. Kelley may have done the right thing by running to tell Judi about Nadia's period, but that didn't mean she wouldn't have to pay for embarrassing her.

Kelley shrugged. "I had to," she said.

"It was *awful*," Nadia said, turning back to the rest of the group. "The worst thing you could possibly imagine."

Jamie's stomach flipped. All the women in her family had gotten their first period super young. Of course, she had more muscle than all of them, but still. She didn't know if she'd be lucky or not and she wasn't ready to find out. She had a sudden urge to curl up on her bed with Chiki, her favorite stuffed animal from childhood, just to prove to the universe she was still too young for puberty.

"I had intense cramps," Nadia continued, "and you *cannot* imagine how bulky a pad is—even the super thin ones. And you have to change them *constantly*.

Nadia spoke as if she were giving expert testimony on a crime show. *Then again, she talks about everything that way,* Jamie thought

"I can't imagine having to wear one with a body suit," said Raven.

"It's like wearing a giant sign that says, 'LOOK AT ME! I'M BLEEDING.'" Nadia confirmed.

Kelley giggled awkwardly. It sounded horrible. Jamie saw how uncomfortable Kelley looked and gripped her hand.

Nadia was talking like she was fine with everything as usual, but for the first time since Jamie had known her, Nadia's eyes looked frightened. Jamie wrapped her arms around her friend and Nadia didn't pull away.

"We hug now?" Nadia said eventually.

"Yes," said Jamie. "We hug now."

"What if I get it during competition?" Nadia whispered into Jamie's hair, her voice small and fragile.

Jamie squeezed her hard then looked her in the eyes.

"Don't worry about that now," Jamie said. "It might not even come back for months. My mom said it's really erratic the first year."

"Great, a few months," said Nadia. "Just in time for Nationals."

The girls shifted uncomfortably, images of bulky pads in body suits, pads falling out of leotards, and worse ran through their minds like the sizzle reel for a bad movie.

"I will *not* compete in front of my friends and family wearing giant diaper!" Nadia declared if forbidding her period from coming again during competition.

Clap, clap, clap.

The girls clapped back in unison.

Jamie had never been so happy to hear that sound. There was nothing she wanted to think about less than getting her period.

She, Raven and Kelley ran over to the beam, where Judi was waiting for them with Sara, who'd come to act as assistant coach today. The symptoms of her OCD, like obsessive hair twirling and hoodie-zipping, seemed to lesson when she was teaching other gymnasts what she knew.

"Raven, this is Sara," said Jamie. "She rocks on beam and uneven bars."

Sara smiled. "Nice to meet you," she said.

"You, too," Raven answered, adding another mental note to her list of weird things about the Bellevue Kips.

"Now," said Judi, "As you know, the trick to beam is staying on. This is usually the make-or-break event at Nationals. There's too much potential for tiny slips and mistakes. Make this your strongest event and you have an edge over the competition."

Nadia smiled confidently. Beam and vault had always been her best events. Her mom had been training her in their basement gym since she was a little kid and they'd been working together since Regionals to bump up her score. A few tenths of a point were all it would take to get her from silver to gold.

Jamie eyed Raven as Judi talked about being comfortable on beam and helped Kelley tape up her ankle.

Raven's dismount on bars bothered Jamie and she couldn't get it out of her mind. It was like a niggling little worm that slowly bored its way into an apple.

We're all Kips, Jamie thought. *It's not really fair for one Kip to have an advantage over the rest of us.*

Not that everyone on the squad had always had equal start values, but it had always reflected their skills and if Jamie could possibly do a fancy dismount, why not let her try?

This is so stupid!

Jamie got frustrated just thinking about it.

I did really well at Regionals. It's not like I haven't proven myself.

Jamie started pacing on the mat. Her whole life had been unique and difficult. Losing her dad when she was really young. Moving from

Miami to live with her grandmother.

A flutter of anxious anticipation rumbled in her stomach. She bounced up and down on her toes to get some of the energy out.

If Judi wouldn't let her do Raven's dismount on bars, maybe she'd let her do something special for beam. It had been a brilliant strategy that came to her while she was brushing out her cat, Baxter's grey and brown hair last night. She'd even downloaded some videos onto her pen drive to show Judi.

"Jamie, what am I talking about?" Judi asked.

Jamie snapped out of her daydream.

"Um, you don't know?" she asked before she could stop the words from tumbling out of her mouth.

Sara burst out laughing.

"Nice one, Jamie," said Nadia.

Jamie brushed an unruly black curl off her forehead. "Sorry Judi, I spaced."

"Focus, ladies," said Judi. "Focus is crucial to balance. And balance is crucial to beam." Judi raised her eyebrows. "Unless you *want* to fall off?" All four gymnasts shook their heads, no.

"And meeting all the requirements, of course," Sara added. "Speaking of which, I have them here." Sara held up a long list of compulsory movements that everyone would have to include in their routine.

"Thank you, Sara," said Judi.

Sara held the paper in both hands as she read. "First off, all of your kicks must be dynamic and high on the arch of your support foot—like demi-pointe in ballet."

"This is where that ballet training comes into play, Miss Nadia," Judi interrupted.

Nadia glowered, but nodded to show Judi she understood.

"Legs straight, body posture and arms extended throughout," Sara continued. "Your leaps must be dynamic, your jumps high. Your posture, perfect, your arms graceful and light."

Judi gave them each her toughest 'you-will-work-extra-hard' stare. The butterflies in Jamie's stomach did a back flip.

"Sara and I will work with you on the specifics of each of the required moves over the course of the next couple of weeks—180 split jump, 180 switch split leap, forward passé turn to horizontal leg hold…"

Jamie bounced up and down. She felt like she couldn't concentrate until she'd said what she needed to say. But this didn't really seem like the right time.

"Standing back tuck, full turn, back walkover, Needle kick, sissone, front walkover or front handspring, back handspring series, and of course, your dismount."

"Ooh, ooh," Jamie's hand shot up in the air. The words were out of her mouth before she even realized she was talking. "I researched some innovative mounts and dismounts. I have videos. I wanted to incorporate one of them into my routine. I thought I could—"

Judi took Jamie's smart phone and the Kips huddled around it.

On the screen, a gymnast did a variation on a side gainer, landing beside the beam instead of in front of or behind it.

"I thought I could change it up by doing a series of back flips right before," Jamie said. "Or an extra twist."

Judi nodded concentrating.

"Good thinking, Jamie." She looked up. "The entire team will work this dismount on the practice beam until we get it. This will definitely give us an edge in the team competition."

Jamie's eyes opened wide. Her heart sank. She couldn't believe what she was hearing. These were *her* moves. *Her* work.

"Everyone can't have the same signature move," she whispered, but no one heard her. "It's not fair."

"This is a good opportunity to work on our building blocks first," Judi said. "We'll all practice a basic side gainer. Once we've mastered that, we'll add-on elements."

Jamie felt deflated. She moaned to herself. *Great, I just handed Judi a teachable moment.*

"Jamie, since it was your idea, you start."

Judi had Jamie stand on the beam. "Start by doing a side gainer somersault in a tuck position. Then we'll do it from the layout position."

Jamie felt like throwing her sweaty towel at Judy but she tried to keep her face happy so no one else would know.

With a gainer, she'd have to travel forward and sideways to avoid smacking her body against the beam. To do that, she'd have to lean in the direction she wanted to move. Balance was crucial.

Jamie stood with both feet resting on the beam. She found her balance by swinging her right foot slightly. When she was ready to move she shifted her weight to her right leg, kicking her left foot back. In the same moment, she moved her arms upward and her support leg, her right, pushed off sending her up in the air but tilted off to the side, like a straight line drawn on an angle. She used the momentum to propel her into two simple back somersaults. She bent her knees on the landing to absorb the impact.

Easy.

"Good," said Judy. "Next."

One after another the gymnasts practiced and mastered the basics.

Judi kept adding moves as they went along, like a game, until one by one the squad started having a hard time.

"I can't seem to tuck in time," said Raven.

When it was Kelley's turn, she bobbled the landing and cried out in pain. Hobbling off the mat, she said, "I see how you can do the somersaults, but I get all messed up when I have to add the twists."

"I'll show you how to correct that," Sara offered.

"Kelley, why don't you sit out," said Judi. "That's enough dismounting on that ankle for one day."

"I'll do it into the pit!" Kelley offered.

"I'll give you ten more minutes, then I want to see you on ice."

Kelley groaned and hobbled away with Sara, just as Raven slipped and landed on her butt.

"Argh! This is so hard!" she whined.

Jamie felt a pulse of glee. Raven wasn't hurt and she couldn't get the dismount.

Jamie on the other hand was determined. She'd moved on to a higher beam in no time, landing in a foam pit. She seemed to know naturally just how hard she had to swing up with her free leg to get the right rotation.

By the end of the day, Nadia was the only other gymnast who could do the variation on a side gainer—and do it with ease.

Of course, Jamie thought.

"Nice dismount, Jamie," Nadia said. "Really creative, I never would have thought of it."

Then don't use it! Jamie was frustrated with herself for being frustrated. It wasn't like her to compare herself to anyone else.

"That's enough for today, girls." Judi ended practice at 6:45 on the dot. "Nadia, Jamie, you can both use the dismount at Nationals if you like. The rest of you, we'll try something else."

Jamie felt a sudden twinge of panic. If she was totally *totally* honest with herself, Nadia performed it better.

I'll just have to convince her not to use it, Jamie thought.

"Saved," said Raven as she walked past Jamie on her way to the locker room.

"Huh?" said Jamie, distracted.

"No lip sync for you today. You totally kicked my butt."

"Thanks!" Jamie forced the corners of her mouth up into a smile, but she was a gymnast with a mission. She scurried ahead to catch up to Nadia.

"It's pretty risky to try a new move so close to Nationals," Jamie suggested as she and Nadia stretched out and got ready to go home. "There's like no time to clean it."

Nadia raised an eyebrow.

"Are you telling me you can't handle it or trying to convince me not to do it?" Nadia always cut to the chase.

"I just want to do something unique," Jamie said.

Nadia gave Jamie her signature blank stare. It always made words spew out of Jamie's mouth.

"Ugh! It is impossible to know what you are thinking!"

Nadia tilted her head to the side.

"You wouldn't want to use the same dismount as me anyway, would you?" Jamie went on. "And I'm definitely using it. I mean, I found it."

Nadia allowed the tiniest hint of a smile to play at the corners of her mouth.

"Let's see how it goes," Nadia said. With that, she casually tossed her gym bag over her shoulder and headed out to the parking lot, leaving Jamie to wonder what had just happened.

"What is that supposed to mean?" Jamie asked.

Nadia stopped and turned in the doorway.

"You wouldn't understand," Nadia said. "It's a woman thing."

* * * * * * * * * * * * * * * * * * *

7:25 p.m.

Raven sat waiting outside the gym—*again.*

Today is mom's day to drive me, she thought. I can keep it straight. *Why can't they?*

She pulled her arms tight around her body. It had started to drizzle again and without the sun to warm things up, Seattle was actually quite cold. But Raven refused to call her mom and remind her. If she was too busy to worry about her only daughter—

Footsteps echoed on the pavement behind her.

Judi.

Great, just what I need, thought Raven.

"No ride?" Judi asked. "Have you tried calling your father's cell?"

Raven shrugged. "My dad said it was my mom's turn."

7:35

Judi pulled out her own cell phone and dialed Raven's mom.

"No! Don't—"

"I do not have time to wait around with you tonight," Judi said. "Hello, Ms. Taylor, This is Judi. Yes, the gymnastics coach."

Raven heard a woman's high-pitched voice on the other end, talking rapid fire.

"I see. I see. Yes. No problem. I'll wait here with her." Judi pocketed her smartphone and looked at Raven. In her most tactful coach voice, she said, "It seems there's been a miscommunication. Your mother was under the impression you'd be staying at your father's. She's on her way."

Grrrrrrrr, Raven did her best to stifle a scream, but she couldn't hold back the tears that had welled up in her eyes. *Figures. Just figures. She held her lips tight and her jaw jut out.*

By the time her mom pulled up in their beat-up old mini-van half an hour later, Judi was annoyed and Raven was sulky and teary.

"There's my baby!" her mom said in that overly cheerful way that meant she was really busy and hadn't planned to spend her whole night driving around.

"Thanks for sticking around," Raven said to Judi as she got in the car.

She sat down, slammed the door shut, and immediately turned her entire body away from her mother, leaning her head against the window.

"I'm always happy for extra girl time," her mom said, placing a hand on Raven's knee.

But Raven didn't buy it.

Neither of her parents seemed to have any time for her lately.

And Raven had had enough.

CHAPTER 8: PARENT PROBLEMS

Raven shoved her books in her locker after second period and caught a whiff of her grimy gym clothes.

"It smells like homeless person in your locker," her friend, Anika teased. Then, Anika leaned in and sniffed the air around Raven's wrinkled prep school uniform. "Smells like homeless person out here, too," she laughed.

"Seriously." Raven huffed and turned to her friend. "I was supposed to stay at my dad's, but he bailed, so I had to stay at my mom's where I had no clean uniform and no washer/dryer. My gym leotard is rancid. Of course! I only sweat it in for about four hours yesterday and—"

Anika cut her off by placing both hands on her shoulders.

"Deep breaths, Rave. Deep breaths."

Once Raven had cracked a smile, Anika pointed out the rational.

"Just call your dad and have him bring you a clean leotard when he picks you up after school. Problem solved."

Raven's face broke into a full-on smile, the first she could remember feeling for the past few days.

"You are genius," she said.

"I am," said Anika. "Why aren't you dialing?"

"Right."

Raven pulled out her phone and dialed her dad. Straight to voice mail. Anika prodded her to leave a message.

"…it's in my dresser, top drawer on the right," Raven instructed. "Don't forget."

"Now," said Raven, turning back to her friend. "Do you have a plan for getting through Social Studies?"

* * * * * * * * * * * * * * * * * *

Time check. 3:15. No dad in sight.

Raven unlocked her phone.

No text messages.

No voice mails.

Frustrated, she stuffed her cell in her pocket. Thinking better of it, she pulled it back out and dialed her dad at work.

He didn't pick up

She sent him an angry text. <<Where are you?>>

Ten minutes later, her mom rolled up.

"Again?!" Raven snapped.

"Don't you snap at me, young lady," her mother said in her most stern voice. "If you are angry with your father, you take it up with him when he picks you up tonight."

"*If* he picks me up tonight!"

Raven crossed her arms and glared out the window as her mom pulled away from the school. "I am going to be *so* late for gym." *And Judi is going to yell at me in front of everyone and probably kick me off the stupid squad.* Bitter tears welled up in her eyes and Raven didn't feel like fighting them. "And I stink!"

"Honey," her mom said, laying a hand on her knee.

Raven shoved it away. "Don't honey me! You're supposed to take care of me." *This divorce is hard on everyone. It's hard on me, too.*

For a moment, time froze. The air in the car buzzed with tension. That kind of acting out did *not* fly with Raven's mother, but she wasn't saying a word. After a few moments, Raven glanced over.

Her mom was crying.

* * * * * * * * * * * * * * * * * *

"You're late, Raven."

Judi didn't even bother to look up from her clipboard. The rest of the squad hovered around the floor mat.

"Take it up with my mom. I don't drive," Raven said in a flat cutting voice. Then she pivoted and walked toward the locker room without waiting for Judi to respond.

"New girl's got fire," Nadia commented as the locker door swung open.

Judi smiled. "Indeed she does."

Just then, Max walked in wearing a shiny black tracksuit with silver stripes running up the legs and arms. The zipper provided just a touch of fuchsia.

"Max!" Jamie cried.

"We're working on our choreography for floor today," said Judi. "I hope you're all ready."

"That's right," said Max in his slight British accent. He clapped his hands together in anticipation. "It's time to take your routines to the next level.

Floor routines were the closest thing to full-on dancing in artistic gymnastics events. They were a solid mix of dance and acrobatic moves—which made them really challenging. Most girls tended to be strong in one or the other—not both.

Like everything in gymnastics, it was all about balance.

Nadia's spine stiffened. She knew Max was going to work her hard on artistry today. She'd always been the top contender on the team, but lately that tenth of a point deduction on her artistic scores had really been holding her back.

Kelley leaned over close to Nadia's ear. "You've got this," she said. "Just show Max what we've been working on."

Nadia looked more annoyed than grateful.

"Remember," said Max. "Floor is as much about showmanship as skill."

"Hmpf!"

Max couldn't help but laugh at Nadia.

"You've got to sell it, Divine Miss Nadia," he said, as he took her hand, pulled her to her feet, and twirled her around until she smiled. "Everyone in the audience should be looking at you and if they're not, you're doing something wrong. Most deductions don't come from acro. They come from everything in between, so confidence, confidence, confidence."

"Thank you, Max," said Judi. "Today's theme is tweaking, Kips. We are going to pinpoint your problems and practice til they're gone. Kelley, you're up first. I want everyone else watching and stretching."

Kelly nodded and headed to the floor. When the familiar twang of the country beat filled the gym, she groaned. She couldn't help it. She liked her routine. She loved Max. But she HATED country music.

Always have. Always will, she thought.

She wanted something more techno. Maybe a little hip-hop. Something that would really let her show-off what she knew. She had a USB drive in her bag with the perfect song on it. She'd wow Max with her performance first, then bring up the idea later on.

Kelley raised her arms into her starting position and launched into her first dance sequence. But after yesterday's tumbling, her ankle was sore. *No way can I hide this from Judi.*

"You will get a deduction for that, Kelley!" Judi called. "I want you to mark the tumbling passes instead of doing them. Just stick with the timing and move across the floor. No jumping. No tumbling."

"She keeps re-injuring," Raven whispered to Jamie. "If she doesn't take a break, she's not going to be able to compete."

Jamie bit her lip. She'd to have a chat with her friend. Kelley would listen to her.

"Raven, let's see what you've got," Judi called out. Kelley hustled off the floor with no time to talk to Max.

"Wish me luck!" Raven said as the girls passed each other.

"Break a leg," Kelley said, mentally kicking herself for missing her chance with Max.

Jamie held her breath. *I wonder what crazy creative combination she has worked into this routine.*

Raven knew she didn't really need luck. She had a lot of energy and she wanted to prove herself. She was late to practice because of her parents. Not because of anything she had done. She was serious about gymnastics. And she was serious about winning. And if she couldn't prove that to her coach and squad by showing up on time, she would prove it on the floor.

Prepare to be floored, she thought. She put on her show face. Confident. Pleased with herself. Ready to impress the audience.

Raven handed Judi a USB drive with her music and took her starting position on the floor mat.

Within a few seconds, her music started playing.

"Is that—Is that like bagpipes?"

"I hear an accordion"

"This is really weird."

"Like Garcia Rodriguez tumbling to the Legend of Zelda theme *awesome*-weird?" Jamie asked. "Or like when that girl at last year's Optionals did hers to "My Heart Will Go On" *awful*-weird?"

"Definitely *awesome* weird," Kelley said, readjusting her ice pack so she could stand and watch. "I mean, just look at her. She's tumbling to Irish folk music and I'm totally into it. I'd actually clap along if I didn't have to hold this ice pack."

Nadia didn't say anything, but she did start clapping. Raven heard it from the mats and added an extra bounce to her step.

Got em, she thought.

The girls were enthralled by Raven's energy.

As she did her second dance passage, a complicated combination of kicks and spins called the Jota, she passed her friends and winked at them.

"I feel like we should be holding hands and dancing in a circle," Jamie said. "Can she win with this?"

"She sure can," said Nadia, impressed.

Just then, Raven did her first tumbling pass. Instead of pausing to take a breather, which is what most gymnasts would do, Raven held her hands by her sides, and began doing a series of intricate footwork and kicks, Riverdance style, that quickly transitioned into a front flip.

Then she hurdled to two front handspring stepouts to a front handspring with her legs together and finished with a rebound.

She was following the guidelines set up by the gymnastics committee for Nationals, but every move she made seemed fresh, original, and entirely her own.

"Her footwork is incredible," said Kelley.

Raven followed up a Double Arabian. The second her feet met the floor, she leapt out of it.

"Full twisting double back piked," said Nadia as Raven landed without the slightest bobble.

"That is so *so* hard!" said Kelley.

"Her start value must be like a 6 at least," Jamie added.

"Her execution," Kelley started. "It's, it's…like, wow."

"Don't you think that's a little extreme?" Jamie asked. "She's good, but— Whoa. Okay, it's very *very* good."

Jamie lost her words as Raven did a 2 ½ straight front.

The music transitioned. It was still Celtic, but now it was contemporary too, with a drumbeat kind of like rock-and-roll. Raven went down into a double spin, and then pushed off against the mat to push up with her toe.

Her leap series was impeccable and her second dance passage was everything the judging committee had asked for with extra energy and style.

"She's a professional," said Nadia, with the hint of a smile. "We have a shot at the team all-around gold with her on our squad."

Jamie looked at Nadia, stunned. She held her jaw tight and didn't say a word.

Here final tumbling run was full of height and when she landed; she stuck to the floor like glue.

"That was the most totally original and gutsy floor routine I have ever seen," Jamie said, her shoulders slumping. Her voice sounded deflated. Kelley instinctively rubbed her back.

Raven landed her final move and smiled radiantly at Max and Judi as if they were the judging committee. The rest of the squad swarmed around her as she walked off the mat.

Nadia was the first to congratulate Raven. "Nice work, Newbie," she said.

Jamie felt stung. *That was always Nadia's nickname for me*, she thought.

Nadia must have noticed because she calmly turned to Jamie and said, "What? You're not the newbie anymore. You're an old-timer like us."

Raven's face broke into a smile. Her cheeks were red and glowing from the exertion and for the first time all day she felt happy.

"Thanks!" she said.

Nadia looked her in the eyes and smiled. "Welcome to the squad."

* * * * * * * * * * * * * * * * * *

Raven left the gym on a high note. She felt like she had finally, *finally* won Judi over. And Max's tweaks to her routine were kind of awesome.

She couldn't wait to tell her dad—to show him that extra driving was worth it.

She ran outside and scanned the parking lot.

No dad.

Why do I even get my hopes up?

No way was she going to risk Judi seeing her and getting annoyed again. Not today.

Raven walked around to the side of the building and plunked herself down on a bench to wait. And wait and wait and wait.

After about twenty minutes, she started to get cold and grumpy.

After about twenty-five minutes, the quiet and shadows and random distant sounds of car doors slamming made her feel like a target.

Mental note: Watch less CSI.

After thirty minutes, she tried her dad's cell. No answer. She didn't even bother to leave a message.

After thirty-two minutes, she called her mom. Straight to voice mail.

"Argh!" In frustration, she stormed toward the gym doors and tried to go back inside.

Locked.

Raven tugged on the heavy glass doors one more time, just in case.

Then she started yanking and kicking them. She screamed at the top of her lungs. Her face was splotchy from crying.

If anyone saw me, she thought. *This is so…so…ugly.* She kicked harder. Screamed louder.

Whatever. I don't care.
Raven looked frantically around the parking lot for Judi's car. Gone. The lot was empty.
She was all alone.
Panicked now, she ran around to check the back door, but she got scared halfway to the other side. *This is one of those situations you think you're too smart to get into,* she thought, *until you're here alone in an isolated parking lot at night and someone pops up out of the bushes.*
Her heart pounding in her chest, she quickly made her way to the front of the building where there were at least big street lights. Her thumb was poised to speed-dial 911.
Just as she stepped into the last shadowy patch, her cell phone rang, nearly making her pee her pants.
"What?" she snapped.
"Hello Sweetie, I got caught up at work. I'm on my way."
"Don't call me Sweetie!" Raven nearly threw her phone at the glass gym doors.
She huddled up in the well-lit doorway and waited for her father to show. *Can't even listen to my stupid iPod,* she thought. If someone was going to sneak up behind her, Raven wanted to hear them coming.
Twenty-mintues later, her dad pulled into the lot.
He's not even speeding.
"I'm so sorry, honey," he said as Raven opened the door. "I—"
"I could have been kidnapped—or worse." Raven slammed the car door. "What? Do you think if you keep forgetting, you won't have to pick me up ever?" She crossed her arms over her chest and bitter, angry tears fell into her lap.
"I—"
"Save it," she snapped.
Her dad tried to apologize again but Raven was not having it. She faced the window, put her earbuds in and turned the volume way up.
Two minutes into their drive, her phone rang.
<<MOM>> popped up on the screen.
Raven unlocked the screen and hit speaker. "Don't stress," she said. "He *finally* showed."
Her mom started screaming.

"Now wait a minute," her father said, "that is not fair."

"Am I on speaker phone?" her mother screeched. "Raven, how many times have I told you *not* to put me on speaker, ever."

"Don't start shouting at Raven, now," said her dad.

The two adults argued for a minute, one raising their voice higher than the other. Raven tried to block it out, but the whole situation just made her more and more stressed. She felt like a bag of microwave popcorn about to burst.

"ENOUGH!" she screamed. She turned to her dad. "Enough, enough, enough. Whatever is wrong between you two is between you two. Stop taking it out on me."

"We're not—"

He pulled the car over to the side of the road, too distracted to drive.

"It. Is. Affecting. Me!" Raven said firmly. "I was just waiting alone and cold in the rain in an empty parking lot."

"Where was your coach?" her mom's tinny voice interrupted over the speaker phone.

"I am not her responsibility," Raven said. "I am yours. You don't get out of daughter duties because you're going through a divorce." Raven slunk down in her seat and hugged her knees. "The screaming. The fighting. The forgetting me has got to stop."

Raven was sobbing now, her shoulders shaking violently up and down.

"Baby," her dad reached for her shoulder but she pulled it away, gasping for air.

Her father watched her helplessly. Her mother was silent.

Finally, her mother broke the tension. "We'll go to a family counselor," she said.

"We'll figure it out."

Family? Raven thought. *Some family.*

CHAPTER 9: UGGH

When Jamie showed up for practice the next day, Kelley, Nadia, and Raven were already sprawled out on the mat, crowded around Nadia's smartphone.

Jamie felt a pang of jealousy.

She took a deep breath, trying not to feel like she'd been replaced.

Ugh! I hate this. Jamie thought. *They can't be excluding me. I just got here!* Jamie put a big smile on her face and walked toward her friends. *I really hope I'm not getting my period, too.*

Jamie had stayed up late the night before practicing her dismount off the living room sofa until her mom made her stop, worried she might break something—like her leg. Jamie's brain spun all night trying to brainstorm new twists and possibilities.

Her grandma was sick in bed with a cold. And even though it was just a cold and not cancer like before, seeing her grandma like that still terrified Jamie.

I'm just oversensitive because I'm tired, Jamie thought. She yawned and stretched to test out her theory. *Yep, definitely tired.*

Kelley popped up off the mat and ran over to her.

"You have *got* to see this!" she said, grabbing Jamie by the arm. "We're getting new warm-up suits for Nationals. Lululemon-style! We finally convinced Judi."

"They're, like, *really* cool," Raven confirmed.

Jamie couldn't tell if Raven's smile was genuine or fake.

Kelley dragged Jamie over to the mat and pulled her down toward Nadia's phone. Jamie looked at the photo of the suit on the screen. It was spectacular.

Nadia slid her fingers across the screen to make it bigger.

"Whoa," Jamie said. The suit took her breath away. It was mostly black with fuchsia and silver piping down one arm and one leg. "It's amazing."

Then Jamie looked at the price tag. She almost choked.

"And we've all agreed to get silver sparkly Uggs to match," Raven said.

"Or Ugg-ish," Kelley corrected. "Uggs are pricey."

Jamie squeezed Kelley's hand, grateful. Kelley knew the situation. The whole reason Jamie and her mom had moved in with her grandma was to cut-back on costs.

There was *no* way she was going to be able to pay for the tracksuit *and* the boots. Her mom had a job at Microsoft, which sounded fancy, but it didn't really pay that much. Plus, there were the parts of her grandma's doctor bills that health insurance didn't cover. It would have taken her mom three paychecks to save up for her new team leotard if her friends hadn't ended up chipping in to buy it for her birthday.

"But they last forever," said Nadia. "We're on the West Coast, but it still gets cold here."

"We're meeting at the mall tomorrow to go shopping," Raven said, filling Jamie in.

"You've already decided?"

Jamie checked the time. She hadn't even been late. When had they made this plan? *Deep breaths,* she reminded herself. *You're just thinking crazy cause you're tired.*

"You can make it, right?" Kelley looked at her with puppy dog eyes. Jamie knew it meant a lot to Kelley that the whole team got along.

"Um, sure," said Jamie, but her head was spinning and the butterflies seemed to have set up permanent camp in her stomach.

"It's all kind of pricey, don't you think?"

"I'm pretty sure I can get my dad to buy mine," Raven said. He owes me."

"I have birthday money," said Kelley. She bit her lip as the boots became a real possibility in her mind. "And I've wanted them forever. They'd be great to slip on after soccer games."

"And they'll fit over your gimpy fat ankle," Nadia teased.

Kelley shot her a dirty look.

"Then it's settled," said Nadia. "We'll meet at the mall tomorrow and look for deals. Good?"

"Good," said Raven and Kelley in unison.

"Good," said Jamie, but all she kept thinking was *bad, bad, bad.*

* * * * * * * * * * * * * * * * * *

That night, Jamie pulled her entire desk over to her bedside so she could lay on her stomach while surfing the internet on her desktop computer.

Her cat settled into the small of her back for a nap.

"Son carisimas, XX," Jamie told the cat she'd had since she was in second grade. "And I don't really need them. I have the boots Alex gave me back in Miami.

Mrrroau.

"I know! It's not right." Jamie said sat up and googled "Uggs" and "Sale." She held her breath while the options came up. It was the wrong time of year for bargains.

"Even Overstock is more than $80," Jamie whined.

Mew.

Jamie sat up, upsetting Axter, and checked the money stash in her night table. Ten dollars including the pile of pennies. She watched her cat jump off the bed and up onto her dresser.

Jamie's mom peeked her head in the door. "Why so sad, *mi princesa?"*

Jamie patted the bed so her mom would sit next to her. "The squad wants to get matching Uggs for Nationals. The tracksuit is pricey enough." She rested her head in her mom's lap.

Her mom frowned and stroked Jamie's curly black hair. "And what do you want to do?"

"I have those gray boots Alex gave me last year," Jamie said. "If it snows or rains, I'll be fine in those."

"Wise. So what do you think you have to do?"

"Be honest with my friends and don't cave to pressure?"

Jamie's mom smiled. *"Que lista, mi hija,"* she said. "So smart. Just like your Mami."

* * * * * * * * * * * * * * * * * * *

The next day, the squad met at the mall. Usually Jamie didn't mind being different, but something about Raven's confidence and abilities—even the style of her bandanas—made Jamie feel weirdly lesser-than lately.

I actually feel nervous being at the mall – with my friends, Jamie thought. *This is insane!*

"Okay, let's get this over with," Nadia said. "We have practice in an hour."

"We'll need ice cream first," said Kelley.

"Ice cream?" Nadia asked.

"For strength," Jamie clarified.

"Yeah, bargain hunting is hard work," Raven agreed and gave Jamie a reassuring smile as if she could tell Jamie felt awkward.

Jamie fingered the ten-dollar bill in her pocket. It was definitely not enough for boots, but it would buy her a pretty massive sundae.

Her mouth watered just thinking about it.

"Make it frozen yogurt and I'm in," said Nadia.

"Done," said Raven. She wrapped an arm across Nadia's shoulder as they headed toward the food court.

"The cafeteria at my school just installed a fro-yo machine," Raven told them. "There have been ten-minute lines for the past week."

"So what's it like to go to private school?" Kelley asked.

"Same trauma, only we have to suffer in uniforms."

The girls spent the next hour running from fro-yo to the sports shop to the make-up store. The mall was packed with people. The buzz reminded Jamie of the way the arena sounded during competition, except the mall smelled like a combination between fresh-baked cinnamon buns and perfume.

"Get that blush brush away from me!" Kelley warned, as Jamie came at her with Mystic Mauve. "I hate makeup!"

"We know," said Nadia. "You complain about it at every competition."

"Well, I hate it at every competition."

"We should get out of here anyway," said Nadia. "We're wasting time."

Finally, Nadia dragged them into a discount shoe store.

"Look at those cleats!" Kelley shrieked. "Turquoise with red stripes." She had had to cut back on soccer practices in order to train for Nationals, but she'd never stopped playing. And she'd never stopped wanting to be the best striker in the league.

"When you can wear them on beam, you can buy them," Nadia said, always the mother of the group.

"What a great idea! I'll do my routines in cleats," Kelley joked. "They don't deduct for that, do they?"

"Har, har," said Nadia, dryly.

"Here they are," said Raven. She picked up a pair of sparkly silver wooly boots and Jamie felt a pang of yearning in her chest. They looked warm and comfortable and stylish at the same time. The images of five different outfits she could wear them with popped into her head. She didn't need Uggs, but she wanted them.

"Look, only $90." Raven said. "That's an amazing a deal!"

The store clerk came over to measure the girls' feet. Everyone pulled off their sneakers except Jamie.

"Two size fours and one size three."

Jamie's butterflies were back, doing somersaults in her stomach.

"Your turn, James," said Kelley.

Just tell them, she thought. *They're your friends. Tell them tell them tell them.*

Her friends stared at her, waiting.

"There are holes in my socks!" Jamie finally blurted out. "I don't want to take my sneakers off!"

Kelley examined Jamie's face, trying to understand what was going on.

"Why did you wear socks with holes in them when you knew we were trying on boots?" Nadia asked.

"Don't be silly, they give you socks to try the boots on with," Raven tossed her a pair of store socks and Jamie felt like she had no choice but to let the clerk measure her feet.

"There are no holes in those socks," Nadia said.

Nothing gets past her.

"No, but they are a little dirty," Kelley teased.

Jamie stepped on the metal thing that measured size and pushed her toes forward.

"Size four."

"Oh my god, we're like, all the same size!" she gasped. Then she crossed her fingers behind her back. *Maybe there won't be enough.*

"I hope they have enough boots," Kelley said, worried.

Kelley gave Jamie a nervous smile. She was so happy just to be with her teammates. It was obvious that Kelley would buy ten pairs of boots if it meant no more drama on the squad.

Jamie smiled back—for Kelley.

I can't be the one who starts tension just when everyone is starting to get along, she thought.

The clerk came back carrying one box.

"Sorry ladies, I only have one size 3 left."

There was a collective groan, but Jamie's eyes lit up.

Tragedy averted, she thought.

"We'll just have to try online," Nadia said and Jamie's heart sank again.

She caught Raven looking at her funny.

"I have a fabulous idea." Raven said, still sizing up Jamie. "Let's get shiny silver legwarmers instead. Then we can show them off in the auditorium, too." She held up the sample silver boots. "These are going to be dirty brown from all this muddy Seattle rain within a week."

Jamie could have sworn she saw Raven wink at her.

She caught Raven's eye and mouthed two little words, "Thank you."

CHAPTER 10: ROTATIONS

"So, like, if you all have to wear the same thing, do you, like, make yourself stand out with accessories and stuff?"

"Have you *seen* my bandana collection?"

Jamie and Raven were chatting on the warm-up mats when Kelley walked into practice the next day.

Finally, Kelley thought. She walked on her heels toward her friends. It was a great strategy for strengthening her ankles. Halfway there, she switched to her toes.

Kelley felt caged up and awful. Normally, if she felt this way, she'd go for a run or dribble a soccer ball against the wall. But her ankle was still sore. She couldn't believe it could hurt for so long.

What do other people do when they feel like this? Kelley wondered. *Nap?*

Kelley dumped her fuchsia bag next to her friends and shook out her shoulders.

No soccer and no tumbling for the past three weeks, she thought. *Bleh!*

It was getting to her. Kelley had kept up her strength training and stretching, but she was used to running around. She liked when her body felt strong and healthy. Now she just felt sluggish and weak.

At least Jamie and Raven seem to be getting along.

Kelley put her arms out to balance and began her favorite ballet warm-up, a series of *rondejons* and *tondu.* They were moves designed to strengthen and lengthen all the small balancing muscles surrounding a dancer's joints.

Well, at least all my bones are in alignment, she thought.

Kelley sat down beside Jamie and started drawing the alphabet in the air with her left ankle, just as Nadia burst through the gym doors.

"Hey, Nadia!" Jamie called. "We're working rotations today."

"Uh-huh." Nadia blew right past her friends and marched straight to Judi's office.

"What is her problem?" Raven asked.

"Do you think she's sick?" Jamie's voice was concerned.

"She probably just forgot her gym clothes." Kelley switched to her other ankle and drew the alphabet backwards this time.

"Hey, guys." Bethany joined her friends on the mat. "Guys? Earth to Kips. Earth to Kips."

"Sorry, we're all just worried about Nadia," Kelley explained. "She's kind of cranky today."

Bethany rolled her eyes, just as Nadia walked out of the office with Judi.

The girls did their warm-up run and got started on rotations. Nadia's mood didn't lighten. She pushed her way to the front of the rotation on vault and criticized everyone's dismounts on the uneven bars.

Jamie tried to add a flip to her transition from high bar to low and Nadia nearly snapped.

"You know you need more momentum if you want to get two flips in!"

"Um, are you okay?" Jamie asked her.

"I'm fine," snapped Nadia, "What's your problem?"

"It's just that you've been kind of snippy all day," Jamie explained. "It's getting a little...hard to deal with."

Nadia stared Jamie down. "You are all ruining my concentration," she huffed as she marched ahead of them toward the mats to work her floor routine.

Bethany laughed and wrapped an arm around Jamie's shoulder. "Come on, I'll show you guys this cool move we learned in aerials class," Bethany said once Nadia was out of earshot. Then she stopped dramatically and turned toward her squad-mates. She pulled her shoulders back into an exaggeration of perfect posture. "Just, you know, make sure you've got enough momentum or you'll never get two flips in."

Jamie couldn't help but giggle. Bethany's Nadia-impersonation was perfect.

"Wait, how long has it been since her last period?" Bethany asked.

"I don't know," said Raven. "But the last time she acted like this, she got her period the next day."

"I sure hope that's it," said Kelley. "At least then we know she'll be nice again in a few days."

CHAPTER 11: ATTENTION TENSION

"Judi, do you think I could work my final tumbling pass on floor with you today?"

It was Bethany's second practice of the week and she felt like she still couldn't get Judi's attention. Nationals were only a week away and Judi was focused on the competition.

"Give me ten minutes, Bethany," Judi said. "I've got to get Raven's dismount polished for Nationals."

Bethany pouted. *I've got a competition coming up,* too, she thought. As soon as Judi turned toward her, Bethany put on her best fake smile.

With my luck, she'd just tell me I can't come to practices anymore. It wasn't a battle Bethany felt like fighting.

Jamie walked up beside Bethany and stretched out her quad muscles.

"Don't stress about it. I've been trying to get her attention all day," she said. "Hey, I could use your help with my beam dismount."

Bethany pouted again. "Only if you'll spot me on mine."

"Of course," said Jamie. "I kinda have to get in all the practice I can get. It's a new dismount, you know."

"Risky so close to competition, no?"

Jamie shrugged. "What you don't think I can handle it?"

Nearby Raven and Judi were working on the uneven bars. Raven's dismount wowed Jamie every time.

"I need something unique if I want to medal, too," she said.

Bethany looked over to where Raven was getting back up onto the low bar. Judi was spotting her and working out the minor kinks, her eyes gleaming with the look of approval all the girls worked for.

"This wouldn't have something to do with the new girl?" Bethany said, an edge in her voice.

Jamie hesitated for a second. She had Bethany had never been close, but Jamie didn't know who else she could talk to about this. Nadia would just tease her and Kelley would worry that Jamie was causing unnecessary tension.

"Raven's cool. It's just that—"

"You were the newbie and now that you're not newbie anymore, you don't know where you fit."

Jamie's face lit up.

"Yes!" she exclaimed. "You understand! How did you know?"

Bethany ran a hand through her long blond hair and sighed.

"It's a more common feeling than you think," she said.

"Can you...would you... maybe spot me?" Jamie asked, giving Bethany worried puppy dog eyes.

"Okay, fine, I'll spot you, but stop looking at me like that."

"Thank you SO, SO much, Bethany! You're a life saver! I knew you were the right person to ask." Jamie bounced on her toes and then smothered Bethany in a hug.

I'm the only person you could ask, Bethany thought.

"I just need one more run through," Jamie said. "Then we can head to bars and I'll help you with your aerial moves."

Bethany followed a bouncy Jamie to the low practice beam.

Not holding my breath, Bethany thought.

Nearby, Sara was spotting Kelley on vault. After about half an hour, the girls took a water break. Raven and Kelley pulled on their tracksuits so their muscles wouldn't get cold.

"Nice track suit," Bethany said to Raven as she took a sip of her own special blend of water. Her mom had taught her to put limes and fresh ginger in it. It was just as refreshing as most sports drinks, but with a lot less sugar.

"You like it?" Raven said, smiling. "They're our new suits for Nationals."

Bethany's cheeks flushed bright red. "Wait, are those Lululemon? I've only been begging Judi to okay those since Optionals 2010. This is so typical."

"Angry much?" Raven cut off Bethany's tirade before it reached catastrophic proportions. "Can you please not have a meltdown?"

Raven looked at Bethany and calmly, sizing her up. She was a full foot taller than Raven, with lean muscles and the kind of facial expression that could be snobby or curious.

Bethany sized Raven up, too. She was strong, no doubt about that, but she had dark circles under her eyes that weren't there the last time Bethany saw her and she sort of slumped when she thought no one was looking.

"What's your deal anyway?" Bethany asked. "You look like a stress ball, but you don't strike me as the type that gets nervous about competition. Something tells me you do better under the stadium lights."

Raven smiled shyly.

"Thought so," said Bethany. "So? What's with you then?

Raven sighed. "Let's see, my parents are divorced. All they do is fight over the phone and the meet is the first time they are going to be in the same space since the divorce finalized."

Raven pulled at a string in her tracksuit and almost tore a hole in it. She gripped her water bottle just to give herself something to do with her hands.

"Oh, seriously," said Bethany. "It's your day. Parents can be so tiresome."

"Right?!" Raven nearly shrieked, finally happy to have someone to talk to. "It's *my* day."

"Can't you just un-invite them?" Bethany asked.

"Un-invite my own parents?" Raven had never thought of that.

"Well, if they stress you out?" To Bethany, it was obvious. "Why are they paying so much money for you to compete in gymnastics if they are essentially going to guarantee you a loss?"

Raven tilted her head, thinking.

"My dad is not allowed anywhere near me on competition days," Bethany continued. "I can just see in his eyes that 'oh, my little girl is off to do this scary thing' look. I make him wake up early and sneak off whenever I have to compete so I won't have to see the fear in his eyes."

"You make your father leave his own house?"

"Absolutely!" Bethany put down her water bottle and looked Raven in the eyes. "This is Nationals. This is important. They can't mess this up for you. Not when you've got such a spectacular bodysuit."

Raven grinned. "You know, you're not half bad, Bethany."

"What did you hear rumors?"

Raven shook her head. "When's your first rhythmics competition? I'll come cheer you on."

"Not 'til the fall."

"Too bad," Raven said.

Bethany paused, an idea taking hold in her mind. "But I'm going to do circus camp this summer. There's a performance at the end. You should come to that." *I need something that's just mine, too,* she thought.

"I'll be there."

"Water break's over!" Judi called.

"Gotta go run through my routine…"

"…one more time, I know, I know. Go."

Bethany smiled as Raven jogged off and Kelley ran up behind her.

"Hide me," she whispered. "I have to get away from Nadia. She's in the worst mood today. Do periods last for two weeks?"

"Hers might."

Kelley tossed her empty sports drink bottle in the recycling bin. "Gotta run!"

Bethany followed Kelley over to the vault. A few months ago, just the sight of the vault would have made Bethany break into a cold sweat. It was her most challenging event and her extra-long legs didn't make getting over it any easier.

"Tuck in your butt, Kelley," Sara corrected. "Okay, work six more reps and we'll pick it up tomorrow."

"Mark those moves Kelley!" Judi called. "I don't want you going all out now and thrashing that ankle for Nationals."

"It feels fine," said Kelley brightly putting on her best fake smile.

"How am I ever going to get ready for Nationals if I can't practice any of my moves," Kelley grumbled. "I got more gym training in back when I was playing soccer and taking dance classes!"

"You know how Judy is," Bethany said. "Way overly protective."

"Don't tell," Kelley said, lowering her voice. "But it's not getting better. If it keeps up like this, the first time I do my tumbling run full out won't be until the competition."

"You've got to go easy on it, Kell," Bethany said. "One competition is not worth permanently damaging your ankle."

Kelley looked at Bethany like she wanted to say something, then thought better of it. "I should stretch," Kelley finally said before walking away.

"Can I have my old life back, please?" Bethany complained to no one in particular.

"How you doin' kiddo?" Bethany looked around for the source of the British accent.

"Max!" They greeted each other with double kisses, European-style.

"I have some downtown," he said. "What do you say, we run through your floor routine and talk about ways we can change it up so it works for a rhythmic competition."

"You know rhythmic?" Bethany's voice almost squeaked with excitement.

"Are you kidding?" Max asked. "I trained for the 2006 Olympics."

Bethany's face lit up as she followed him towards the mats.

"Oh, Max," she fake-swooned. "You say all the right things."

CHAPTER 12: TENSION BREAKER

"Look, we have to talk."

After another hour of practice, the girls hit the mats to stretch out their weary muscles. Nadia grabbed Bethany by the upper arm and pulled her aside as the rest of the squad bent into downward dog.

What am I everyone's confessional today? Bethany thought. *I feel like the cameraman on 'The Bachelor'.*

"What is up with you?" she said aloud. "You're not going to try to kill me are you?"

"Of course not. I just need to talk to you."

"And why am I being honored?"

"I need to know something," Nadia said, her green eyes focused on Bethany's like laser beams. "What is it like to NOT be a gymnast anymore?"

"I'm still a gymnast," Bethany said, glaring back.

"No, I mean like not a competitive gymnast."

"I'm still competitive. My rhythmics squad is going to Optionals and …."

Nadia held up a hand to interrupt her. "You know what I mean. You're not competing at Nationals and you don't want to go to the Olympics."

Bethany's eyes flashed for a minute. Then she twisted a strand of her blond hair and slowly calmed down.

"Look, it wasn't an easy decision to stop competing at the same level as you guys—to not go to Nationals with the squad." Bethany paused looking for the right words. "I struggled with it for a long time. I did a lot of research. But once I made that decision, I'm really happy with it." Bethany paused to make sure Nadia was taking her seriously.

"I'm not nearly as stressed out. And I finally remembered what I've always loved about gymnastics. Am I totally jealous that you all waited til I left to get the Lululemon shiny fuchsia team tracksuits I've always been pushing for? Yes, but—"

Nadia looked passed her toward the beam, anxious to get back to training.

"I'd gotten to this place where the thought of competing and failing—of not doing the best, really, really stressed me out," Bethany said. "I didn't even like practices. I was a nightmare to be around."

"We remember," Nadia said.

"Nadia, I still love gymnastics, but now the pressure is off. But if you want my advice?"

Nadia raised an eyebrow.

"You are not me. You thrive on competition. You seem to…like the pressure. I can't see you giving up competition." Bethany watched as Raven left the bars and Kelley jumped on. "Where is all this coming from anyway?"

Nadia looked away.

"I got my period again."

Bethany burst out laughing. "No kidding! Is THAT what this is all about?"

"Keep your voice down." Nadia's cheeks flushed bright red. "I can't compete if I have my period. It's too embarrassing. What if it leaks?"

This time Bethany grabbed Nadia's arm. "And what if it doesn't?" She held Nadia's gaze. "Nadia, women for centuries have done amazing things while they've had their periods. It is not leprosy. But I totally know what you mean. Have you ever read those books about like the world's most embarrassing stories? At least half are about like leaking pads and white skirts."

Nadia pulled away. "This is not helping."

Bethany put both hands on Nadia's shoulders. "Nadia, talk to Judi. Talk to your mom! I can only imagine what it's like. They'll know for sure. They've both lived as super successful gymnasts with their periods and last time I checked, they'd both survived. Besides, I hear exercise is a great cramp-killer."

Bethany winked and Nadia smiled. "You know you're not that bad now that you aren't acting like a walking nightmare," Nadia said.

"No competition, I'm tellin ya." Bethany put her arm around Nadia's shoulder and walked her toward Judi's office. "A stupid fact of life is no reason to give up Olympic dreams."

And not being on the squad is no reason not to get the tracksuit of your dreams.

* *

"See you tomorrow, Raven," Jamie called.

"Catch ya, then!"

Raven said goodbye to her squad and slowly made her way out to the parking lot.

At least Jamie's not acting all mad at me anymore, she thought. She was glad she'd managed to get rid of at least some of the tension in her life.

A car horn toot-tooted. Her mom was in a hurry.

Ooh, my ride's on time.

"Hey," Raven said as she got into the car.

"Good practice?"

"Yep."

Raven stuck in her ear buds and turned her music up as her mom hummed along to the oldies station on the radio.

Their new ritual.

There was a time when Raven couldn't wait to tell her mom all about practice. All the new moves she learned. What she still wanted to learn. What girl said what to whom and in what voice.

But Raven and her mom didn't have a whole lot to talk about lately. Actually, there was so much they *weren't* talking about, Raven couldn't think of a thing to say.

She scratched at an old sticker on the inside of the door, working up the nerve to say what she'd been thinking about since her conversation with Bethany.

She pulled down the sun visor and checked her face in the mirror. She looked tired. But her mom looked a lot worse. Her hair was frizzy. Her clothes were wrinkled. And her nails were bitten down short and stubby.

Raven noticed that she was wearing two different socks.

"You have to make sure you're out in the parking lot at 7 on the dot when I pick you up Raven. I—"

"Fine." *This is not making this conversation any easier.*

"I'm not finished."

"I said fine," said Raven. She paused to build up her nerve. "So…I've been thinking."

Raven's mom braved a glance at her daughter. She knew trouble was coming.

"Since dad is coming to Nationals. And the two of you don't get along. And the fighting really stresses me out. And I'm going to be stressed enough anyway…" Once Raven got started, she couldn't quite control the words coming out of her mouth. "I mean, it is Nationals, I mean. I want to do my best. And there's already all this pressure cuz my new gym is so far and…"

"Raven, honey, what are you trying to say?"

Raven tried to gage her mother's mood by her tone of voice.

Eh, she's never in a good mood anymore anyway, she thought. *Just go for it.*

Raven took a deep breath and let it out through her nose.

"I don't think you should come to Nationals. There's too much fighting. I can't handle it."

Pow. Raven could tell from her mom's silence that she'd taken the comment like a punch to the gut.

Her mom opened her mouth, then closed it again. She licked her lips and bit the bottom one. She looked like she was silently counting to ten.

Raven slunk down a little further in her seat. She couldn't handle all of this tension—always feeling like the bad guy. If her mom wanted to get upset, fine. Raven didn't have the energy.

"I hear what you are saying," her mom finally said. "And I

understand your reasoning."

Raven let herself feel hopeful.

"But we are both your parents and we both want to be there to support you during major moments."

"So...?"

"I think the three of us should all sit down and discuss this," her mom said. "We need to find a way to be civil together. I can't—" her voice broke. "I can't miss the things that are important to you just because your father is there."

"Thanks mom," Raven said feeling suddenly hopeful. She put a hand on her mom's knee. She didn't know what they were going to say to one another.

But she was ready to work on a solution.

CHAPTER 13: FAMILY BALANCE

Jamie balanced on the beam. She completed a pivot turn into a straight jump and landed perfectly, without looking down at her feet. Jamie allowed herself a smile. She felt more like herself than she had in the last few practices.

She was putting a lot of pressure on this event—an event with a big margin for error. But she wanted to win. And she wanted to be unique. A wiggle of anxiety rose up from her stomach and Jamie took a deep breath to push it back down.

Just breathe into each move, she told her body. *We're surfing and we're letting the wave carry us along.* She balanced on her right leg, leaned her chest forward, and lifted her left leg back into a 180 degree split. Then she bent all the way over and grabbed her ankle. She felt at one with the beam now. She didn't need to think about finding her balance as she moved through her routine. She knew it was there. She knew the beam would support her.

"Excellent Scissor Scale!" called Sara from the mats. "Good balance."

Jamie smiled. She loved that Sara had committed to spotting them in this week leading up to Nationals. She loved that helping the squad stay calm helped Sara stay calm.

Jamie felt for the bar with her toe. *Still there,* she thought. *Right where it should be.*

She prepared her body for the variation on a side gainer dismount she was determined to perfect before the weekend's competition. Trying not to think too much about it, she swung her right foot to find her balance.

"That's it," Sara said, moving into position to spot Jamie.

Jamie shifted her weight to her right foot and kicked her left foot back. Soon, she was up in air, angled just right, tilting, twisting and pushing her body into two back somersaults. Jamie felt off-kilter. A bolt of anxiety shot through her body. The mat came up quickly beneath her. Too quickly.

She landed on her heels and slipped backwards onto her sits bone.

"Ouf!" she cried.

Sara rushed forward.

"Are you okay?"

"Yes," said Jamie, putting on a determined smile. "Good thing I don't need to do much sitting during my routines. Ouch." Jamie rubbed her lower back. She was frustrated, but she'd been frustrated before and she'd always mastered the moves that tormented her. There was no reason she couldn't nail this one as well.

"Jamie, that dismount is too much of a gamble this close to competition."

Judi. She wasn't supposed to see that.

Judi's voice was firm. She was in charge and she was making a decision. Jamie's heart sank.

"You're old dismount is fine and clean." Judi said as she walked over and helped Jamie to her feet. "Use that one."

Then, just as quickly, she walked away toward the uneven bars. The conversation was clearly over.

Jamie stood beside Sara and watched Judi walk toward the uneven bars where Raven completed a perfect double flyaway before launching into her spectacular release move.

"I can't use my old dismount," Jamie told Sara. "There's just no way."

Three clear electronic notes rang out and Sara ran over to her bag to check her cell. Her eyebrows pressed together in concern.

"What's up?" asked Jamie.

"It's Kelley," said Sara. "She rolled her ankle playing at recess. She's at home and on ice."

"No!" cried Jamie. "Will she be able to compete?"

"I don't know," said Sara. "I just don't know."

* * * * * * * * * * * * * * * * * * *

"You're late."

"I was in an important meeting."

Raven's dad was late picking her up from practice—*again*. She felt like she was trapped in the movie, *Groundhog Day*, forced to relive the same moment over and over again with only slight variations.

"I need you to be here in the parking lot at seven on the dot when I walk through that door," Raven told her father. Somehow, using her mother's words made Raven feel powerful.

"Raven Eileen Taylor, do not take that tone with me."

"Why? Because you're the Dad?" Raven was having a hard time controlling her temper. "Well then, start acting like one. I have no idea how to get through to you. It is not safe for me to wait here alone and it is not Judi's responsibility to stick around so you can have a meeting."

"My meetings pay for your gymnastics."

"Speaking of which, I've been thinking." Raven didn't hesitate. It was now or never. "You pay so much for gymnastics; it's not worth it for you to blow my shot at a medal by showing up."

"What?" Raven's father jerked the car to a stop at the red light. "What are you talking about?"

Tears started streaming down Raven's cheeks. She gasped for air.

"You obviously don't care about me. So *I* don't care to have you at Nationals."

"Raven, that is absolutely not true."

"Oh, just save it!" Raven snapped, turning her entire body toward the window.

She felt a black hole opening up inside her chest sucking away all the hope that had been there just last night. She didn't think she could ever fill it. And she didn't think a family meeting was going to solve anything.

Now I have no one to come watch me at Nationals, she thought.

No mom. No dad.

No one.

She fiddled with the cord that connected her earbuds to her iPhone.

It's for the best anyway.

Or at least—a giant sob threatened to choke her. *At least I'd better start getting used to it.*

CHAPTER 14: MOCK COMPETITION

Kelley gritted her teeth through the pain as she worked on her floor routine. She'd spent the past two days icing and elevating and she was done with sitting still. It was time to press on.

The dancer in her was happy to be leaping around the mat, using the whole space. She felt the music in her body, moving her muscles and it energized her. Kelly tested her ankle by jumping up into a scissor split.

No pain on the landing.

Good, thought Kelley. *I've got this.* Confident now, she moved into a tumbling run.

This is where the audience starts clapping along, she thought.

Her muscles remembered the moves even though she hadn't fully practiced the routine fully in a while. Pushing down to lift up, Kelley propelled her body into a punch layout front to a second front in pike—one of the required elements for the second pass.

She nailed it.

The squad was clapping, cheering her on. They had decided to spend their last practice before Nationals doing a mock competition to simulate what they'd be going through that weekend. They'd already completed vault and beam and were now halfway through the floor routines. After each event, Judi, Max, and Sara, who were all watching, would give them individual scores and notes for improvement just like on *American Idol.* Kelley would have thought it was funny if it hadn't felt so real.

After all four events, the panel of judges would name one girl winner for the day and she'd get to choose the movies for the bus ride down to Nationals in Salt Lake City, Utah.

Kelley finished her final dance pass into a tumbling sequence and raised her arms high above her head. She felt strong. Her ankle throbbed a bit, but she ignored it. She knew it was going to be swollen by the end of practice, but she'd worked hard for this. And she was ready.

Besides, there was an industrial-sized bag of ice waiting in her freezer at home.

"Good work, Kelley," said Judi. "Make sure you rub some sports cream into that ankle between events."

Nadia struggled to emphasize artistry during her floor routine. It helped when Kelley talked her through it from the sidelines.

"Remember to keep your moves continuous," Kelley called out.

Nadia took two steps forward to a horizontal leg up full turn.

"Keep your arms up on the Tour jeté!" Kelley called.

"Okay, I get it," Nadia snapped and she swung her arms and jumped into a switch split.

Kelley blushed with embarrassment.

Jamie was quick to rub her back. "We're all a little tense, she said. Don't take it personally."

"Yeah, right," Kelley said, feeling a little deflated.

Nadia finished her routine and moved on toward the uneven bars without saying a word to Kelley. This was a mock competition and there was no time to mend relationships between events.

Judi furiously scribbled on her clipboard as the girls moved to the uneven bars and either chalked up their hands or pulled on their grips.

Raven's routine had gotten better and better with every practice.

Jamie watched as Raven did a Pike toe circle to long hang kip handstand, one of the required elements. Raven's legs remained straight through the completion of the circle and the extension of her glide was perfect. She maintained straight arms and a straight body with her legs together throughout the cast and finished in a handstand with a straight body.

Jamie almost couldn't look as Raven performed her totally unique dismount yet again with absolutely no wobble on the landing.

I will use that side gainer dismount on beam, Jamie told herself. *Judi wasn't ordering me not to. It was just a suggestion.*

Jamie was up next. With her grips wrapped tightly, she leapt up to begin her routine on the low bar. Her form was excellent and her bodylines straight on all her swings, but she couldn't help feeling like she wasn't nearly as good as Raven. She didn't feel as light or graceful as Raven looked when she twisted her body and switched hand positions.

Jamie did a pirouette—a handstand on the high bar that changed directions with a twist—before swinging down to the low bar. Her body was perfectly vertical—not even a hair out of place. Back up to the high bar and swing, swing, swing.

Using the momentum she'd built up, Jamie swung her body up and into a handstand, released at the top of the movement, twisted her body in the air with legs straight and re-grabbed the bar facing in the opposite direction.

Jaime swung once, released her grip at the top of the bar opening her legs into a wide split and then grabbed the bar again with her hands between her open legs.

She'd forgotten that the other girls were there. She'd forgotten that it was a competition at all. All she thought about was tucking her butt in, keeping her legs fully extended, and the incredible feeling of flying.

Jamie barely paused between each move. Finally, she swung around once twice three times and then twisted her body in the air on the dismount, her arms crossed over her chest.

Jamie wobbled a little on the landing. Even though most of her routine had been near perfect, she frowned as she walked off the mat.

"Good work, Jamie," Judi said.

"Good work?!" Jamie cried out in frustration. "I wobbled that landing."

"Everyone makes mistakes," Judi reminded her. "How many perfect tens do you see on the scoreboard? Even Gabrielle Douglas messes up sometimes. The trick is how you handle it. Do you let it cause a meltdown or do you accept that no one is perfect and push on?

You've been training for this. Every other competition has been leading up to this." Judi paused to look around at the girls. She was proud of them and it was evident in her eyes.

"As a squad, you are in the strongest position I've seen you in, all year. You have a real shot to metal in team all-around. And some of you may even have a shot at a medal in an individual event."

"Some of us?" repeated Raven.

"May have?" Nadia said, arching an eyebrow.

"You girls are good," Judi continued, "but this is your first time at Nationals. I will be proud if you pull out your best performances so far. You do not have to medal to be successful in this competition."

"Since when?" Nadia asked.

"A good competitor stays calm and focused," Judi reminded them. "She doesn't compare herself to others and feel bad about it. She compares so she can learn. So she can push herself to do better. To perform her best."

"Cue the National anthem," Raven said a little too loudly.

"You know what I mean," Judi said. "You are all competitors in your own way, each and every one of you. And you are all prepared." She looked around at the group of nervous girl faces, the muscular limbs shaking out around her, unable to hold still.

"We need a team chant," Jamie suggested.

"Like a cheer?" Kelley asked.

"Yes, like a cheer," Jamie said. "For ourselves. For team spirit."

Nadia scowled at her. Clearly, she thought this was a waste of time.

"What we really need is a bet," said Raven.

"Not another one." Jamie's heart sank a little. Bets made her nervous. But Raven smiled mischievously.

"And I have the best idea."

CHAPTER 15: MIAMI

"Miss Lucy had a steamboat."

"The steamboat had a bell."

"Miss Lucy went to heaven."

"And the steamboat went to—"

"Look we're here!"

The bus ride to Salt Lake City, Utah had been long. Luckily, too long to be tense or anxious. Judy, Max, the entire squad, along with Kelley, Nadia and Jamie's moms and a friend of Judy's were all loaded into a big rented bus.

They'd taken one rest stop halfway through, but they'd spent the rest of the ride watching all three *Twilight* movies, courtesy of Nadia. Kelley had been surprised by the choice, but Jamie knew Nadia had a girly girl hidden inside her.

"Thank goodness, I was about to lose it!" Raven shouted. "I can't stand Bella."

The bus pulled into the local hotel where other buses just like it were unloading teams wearing all different colored tracksuits.

Kelley wiped a foggy patch clear with her sleeve and looked out the window.

"Is that eight-year-old who kicked our butts on beam at Regionals?"

"I don't know, but look at that squad wearing red, white, and blue."

"So tacky."

"Ick, even their hair ribbons look like American flags."

"Tacky? Why?" asked Jamie's mom. "It's patriotic."

"You shouldn't wear your country's colors until you've earned them," said Nadia.

"You mean until you've medaled in the Olympics?" Jamie's mom clarified.

"Or here," said Nadia's mom.

"Sometimes it's like you girls speak a totally different language," Kelley's mom piped in.

"Sometimes?" Kelley smiled. "Try all the time." Kelly's mom mussed her daughter's hair. It had taken her a while to get on board with all the time Kelley spent training for gymnastics, but now that they'd made a family decision to support Kelley, she was all-in.

"Don't worry," Nadia's mom assured them. "I'll teach you some of the lingo over drinks in the hotel lounge tonight."

"Hey, Raven," Kelley asked. "Is your old squad here?"

"No, they're staying at the Hyatt, but we'll see a few of them tomorrow."

"Anything we should know?" Nadia asked—always pure business.

"They're tough. But so are we."

Nadia nodded.

Jamie's phone vibrated and she pulled it out of her gym bag."

<<HEY HEY JAMIE-GIRL! I SEE YOU!>>

Jamie gripped her mom's hand.

"It's Alex! She's here. She sees us through the window." Jamie ran to the other side of the bus and pressed herself up against the window looking for her Miami friends.

"Look, look, Kelley, there she is! Oh my god!" Her squad from Miami was going to be here at Nationals as well. Jamie was excited to be under the same roof competing with them.

"She looks so stylish," Kelley said.

"And tan," added Nadia. The constant Seattle drizzle and lack of sunshine had been getting to them all.

"For sure!" said Jamie.

A girl in a neon green and black tracksuit waved at Jamie as her squad filed into the hotel. She held up her cell phone for Jamie to see just as a text came in.

<<POOL PARTY @ 6. Be there or be 🐌>>

"We're meeting at the pool at six," Jamie told her squad. "You guys have to come. It'll be so much fun!"

"I'm in," said Raven.

"Me, too," said Kelley.

"We need to stay focused," Nadia reminded them.

"What do you think he other teams are going to do? Try to sabotage our routines poolside?" Raven asked.

Nadia shrugged and Jamie threw a bus blanket at her.

"You're crazy."

A friend of Judi's had volunteered to drive the van. He pulled it into a parking spot and turned off the engine.

"Okay, girls," he said. "Grab your gear."

"We've arrived!" Max finished.

Four tired but excited gymnasts, four achy moms, two coaches, and one driver piled off the van and headed into the hotel. The squad-mates were all staying on the same hallways with their moms. Jamie and her mom with Kelley and her mom to save money. And Raven with Nadia and Nadia's mom.

"I'm nervous," Raven told Jamie as they carried their gear and suitcases inside.

"About tomorrow?"

"No, about staying with Nadia and her mom. They're intense."

Jamie laughed. "Nadia's mom is awesome. If you want last minute prep for competition, she's the one to talk you through."

Raven thought about the rituals she had always had with her own mom before competition. The night before they'd get a mani-pedi with her squad-mates and the other parents so they could feel pampered and special before the competition. She wondered if her friends were at the salon right now with their moms.

"Pool in fifteen minutes?" Jamie asked.

"Wouldn't miss it!" Raven said, forcing herself to be cheerful.

Half an hour later, the Kips descended upon the pool in matching fuchsia and black bathing suits, while the moms all went off together to the hotel lounge.

"Jamie! James!" A high-pitched voice squealed as the girls entered the basement pool area. They dropped their towels on a lounge chair while a girl with a spikey bleach-blond haircut wrapped her arms around Jamie and started shrieking.

"Jamie! Jamie! Jamie! Jamie!"

"Oh my god! Oh my god!" Jamie cried in return.

The girls jumped up and down.

"You look beautiful! I LOVE this swimsuit."

"We wear team colors all the time," Kelley said.

"Well, your team colors are fabulous," Alex said.

"Kelley this is Alex. Alex, Kelley." Jamie introduced her friends, knowing they would love one another.

"Oh my god like Jamie talks about you all the time," Alex said. "I can't wait to see your floor routine."

Kelley wrinkled her nose. "I can't wait to see your vault! I hear you have crazy power."

Alex faked shyness. "Aw, shucks," she said. "I feel like a celeb. Race you to the diving board?"

"Oh my god, can you do a double back somersault off the board?" Jamie asked.

"Can you?" Kelley asked, turning to Alex.

"But of course, darling!"

Kelley, Jamie, and Alex raced off, while Raven and Nadia slowly settled themselves in poolside.

"I'm going to swim laps," Raven told Nadia. "You coming?"

"No, thanks, I'm just going to put my feet in."

Raven shrugged. "Suit yourself."

Nadia watched her friends risking injury to jump off the diving board. She took a moment to stretch out her ankles in the water as Raven swam by, rotating them first left then right. Nadia thought about Nationals tomorrow. She wasn't sure she had improved her artistry enough to be fully competitive, but her acro was better than ever. She felt like she had a shot if she remained focused.

The water felt good on her feet and Nadia began visualizing her vault in her mind. Beam had always been her event, but lately her vaults were getting better and better.

She could almost feel the strength of her legs beneath her as she mentally ran toward the table. She could practically feel the cool leather, her body launching into the air, twirling, twisting, changing direction and…

Oh, she thought. *That's it! I have to be tighter on the launch. My angle's been off. If I can just tighten my abs and squeeze my butt under I bet I'll get a more precise rotation. That'll add a tenth of a point at least.*

"Do you think she has her period?"

"I don't know, but she won't swim and it's freaking me out!"

"She swore she wouldn't compete if she got it. We need Nadia."

The sound of her name in her teammates' stressed voices snapped Nadia out of her daydream.

She stared at her friends.

"I do not have my period. And I do not waste energy swimming before a competition," she declared simply. "Busy yourselves with other things like playing in the pool. The elite athletes here are mentally preparing while you wear yourselves out."

The girls were stunned into silence until Alex laughed out loud.

"Oh my god, you are like a Hollywood star from the 1940s!" Alex cried. "All glamour and sultry seriousness. You're beautiful. I bet you medal tomorrow."

Nadia's cheeks turned bright red, then warmed into a smile.

"I like your friend, Miami," Nadia told Jamie.

Jamie's heart leapt at the new nickname. She didn't have to be the newbie anymore. She was an old-timer, just like Nadia and Kelley. They'd been through at least three competitions together and it felt good.

I have the best squad, Jamie thought. *And the best friends.*

* * * * * * * * * * * * * * * * * *

That night, the girls ate dinner together in the hotel restaurant and talked strategy for the next day. Afterwards, they headed upstairs early to get a full night's rest. The swim had been just what they'd needed after a long day in the bus and now they were all tired.

Raven took a nice hot shower while Nadia and her mom chose a movie on Netflix. When Raven came out of the bathroom in her pajamas, Nadia was already asleep tucked under her mother's arm. mom gently rubbed her scalp. Raven quietly grabbed her cell phone and ducked back into the bathroom.

<<Hello>>

"Hey, mom."

<<Raven!>>

"We're here safe."

<<How do you feel, honey?>>

Raven felt an immense hole open up somewhere in her chest. She felt lonely and guilty and like a part of her was missing. She remembered the last time her mom had come to a competition with her. They'd spent the night tucked under the covers and her mom told her stories about when she was young.

Raven's mom hadn't been a gymnast, but she'd been athletic. She ran track for four straight seasons in high school and she was used to competition. She understood everything Raven was feeling pre-meet. And she'd always given Raven a good perspective on major events.

Then her dad would show up with some surprise dinner he'd driven off to get and make them all laugh. Tears sprang to Raven's eyes at the memory of them as a happy family.

<<Raven?>>

"Oh, fine fine. All good, no worries. Super fun, actually. We spent the afternoon at the pool and everything. I just wanted to check in."

<<Oh.>> Raven heard her mother's voice falter. <<Well, okay then. Good luck tomorrow. I mean, break a leg.>>

"Thanks mom"

<<And Raven? You know I love you.>>

"Yeah mom, I love you, too."

Raven didn't even realize she'd been crying until she hit <<END>>. She brushed her teeth until the tears stopped and then climbed straight into bed without looking at Nadia and her mom in the double bed next to her. She put her cell phone on the night table between them and rolled over to face the wall until she fell asleep.

It's for the best, she thought. *I am so over the whole family scene!*

As Raven's breathing finally regulated and she drifted off into the trace of a snore, Nadia's mom gently rolled out from under Nadia's head and tucked her daughter in. Then she took Raven's phone and checked the outgoing calls list.

Nadia's mom knew what it was like to be a gymnast. She knew competition.

And she had a plan.

CHAPTER 16: THE BIG DAY

The alarm went off early the next morning, jolting Raven out of bed. She reached for her cell to turn it off.

It was way further away than she remembered.

5:45 am

Eesh.

She took one last longing look at Nadia and her mom who were slowly waking up and popped into the bathroom.

It was game day and even though Raven didn't feel like she had anyone in her corner, she was ready to win.

Nadia met her gaze and nodded.

She was ready, too.

I have a squad full of competitors, Raven thought. *They'll be in my corner.*

"We're all meeting in Jamie and Kelley's room to do your hair before you put your leotards on," Nadia's mom told them.

The girls washed their faces and stumbled next door.

"G'morning," said Kelley, sleepily.

"Hey guys," called Jamie, already excited for the competition. There was something about all the preparations that always energized Jamie. As her mom scrunched her kinky unruly hair into long ringlets, Jamie thought about her new dismount.

I can so totally do this, she thought. *I rocked at Regionals. Competition always gets me pumped. This is exactly the moment to try it.* Her stomach fluttered with anxiety as the image of her flubbing the move in practice flashed into her mind.

"I can do this," she said out loud.

"You certainly can, *princesa,*" her mom said as she kissed Jamie's forehead. "I know *mi hija*. And I know what you can do. I'm already proud of you."

Kelley's phone vibrated on the dresser.

"It's Bethany!" Kelley squealed. "She's calling from Skype."

"Answer answer!"

"Bethany!"

Kelley held up the phone so Bethany could see everyone and say hi.

<<Guys! I can't believe I'm not there with you all. You look great! Even you, Nadia.>>

"Ha ha," said Nadia.

<<I wish I could've come with just to watch, but you know I've got to save up for circus camp.>>

"We promise to call you as soon as we know the results," Kelley assured her.

<<I'd wish you luck, but I know you're all going to kill it out there. Even you, new girl. Miss me much?>>

"SO MUCH!" Raven shouted.

"We're not having any fun without you, Bethany!" Kelley cried.

"Yeah, this hotel is *so* incredibly boring." Jamie added.

"Five minutes to breakfast." Judi opened the door and popped her head in. "I want to see you all suited up and downstairs pronto."

"Gotta go, Bethany!" Kelley said.

<<Love you, all!>>

"We love you too!"

The girls put on the finishing touches and headed down to breakfast. They walked into the hotel conference room with sparkly silver eyes and bright pink lips. Fuchsia hair clips added a touch of shimmer to their hair.

"Whoa!" said Jamie when she saw the breakfast buffet. "It' looks like the Olympic village."

At least five different squads were lined up for steaming piles of scrambled eggs and waffles dripping with maple syrup.

"Don't gorge!" Nadia warned.

"What my daughter means to say is that you want to eat healthy before the competition," Nadia's mom corrected. "Remember, you want protein this morning girls. Eggs, bananas for potassium and some granola. Skip the pancakes. You do not want to sugar crash during the competition."

Alex waved to Jamie from across the buffet line. The steam from the food trays made her look like the ghost—the ghost of Jamie's former life here to remind her of her mission—to win gold.

Jamie grabbed a breakfast sausage and ran through her new beam dismount one more time in her mind. She was ready.

Nadia snatched a pancake off Kelley's plate and tossed it in the trash bin. "We're a team."

Kelley closed her eyes and counted to five.

"There was peanut butter on that," she said, looking Nadia dead in the eyes. "The natural kind. An excellent source of protein." Kelley grabbed another pancake and a banana and took a seat. She wasn't going to let Nadia bother her. This was her big day. She hadn't gotten to be with her team at Regionals, but she was here now and she wasn't going to miss even a second of it feeling angry or worried.

Kelley looked around at the sea of shiny blue, pink, silver, black and lime green. And her face broke into a big smile.

Her mom came over and pulled her into a hug. "I see why you love gymnastics so much," she said.

"You haven't seen anything yet."

* * * * * * * * * * * * * * * * * * *

The Salt Lake City convention center auditorium was bigger than any venue Raven had ever competed in. She tried to muster up the enthusiasm she usually felt before competition. She checked in with herself trying to figure out what would explain her lack of energy. It was always hard to sleep in a new bed, but she'd been so tired from swimming she'd had no problem.

New squad? She looked over at Jamie who was fussing with Nadia's hair.

Naw, these guys are cool.

Nationals? Raven thought. *Nup. Same competition. Bigger name.*

No mom and dad? Raven's heart sank. *No. There they are.*

"What?!"

Raven's parents waved to her from the other side of the auditorium. They made their way through the hoards of gymnasts, fans, and press to get to their daughter.

Am I going crazy? She looked over at Nadia and her mom for a reality check. Nadia's mom grinned like she'd just pulled off the surprise of the century.

"You called them?"

"I hope you don't mind," she said. "Sometimes I just think I know best about what a gymnast needs before a competition. My daughter finds it rather annoying."

"No, you were right to call," Raven said. "Thank you."

"Raven!" Raven's mom wrapped her in a big bear hug.

"Sweetness," said her dad.

"Mom! Dad! You're here!" Raven gave them each a big hug, then stood back. "And you're together!"

"And we're on time," her mom couldn't' help saying.

Her dad laughed. "You need family in your corner, Raven," he said. "Whether you realize it or not. And we're not going to let you down. Not anymore."

Raven teared up, but this time out of happiness.

"We spent the whole afternoon at a family counselor yesterday," said her mom.

"We were so relieved when we got that phone call. We really wanted to be here, but we didn't want our issues to distract you."

"I'm so glad you came," said Raven. "Thank you."

<<Group A please report to the warm-up area.>> A deep female voice boomed over the PA system. *All restricted persons please vacate the gym floor.*

"That's me!" said Raven. "Gotta go!" She kissed her parents good-bye and hurried over to join her squad.

"Okay, girls," said Judi. "Take advantage of this time."

"Today we've got floor and vault followed by beam then bars." She looked at them and narrowed her eyes as if trying to transfer her own confidence to each gymnast. "You're ready for this."

"Nadia, you'll be first."

Nadia nodded. She felt more nervous than she usually did before a competition. She'd been working so hard on her artistry. She wanted all that hard work to show in her routine.

By the time the sounds of a techno beat blared through the auditorium, Nadia was in her starting pose on the mat and feeling confident.

I've got this, she thought.

Kelley watched her from the sidelines, willing her to be graceful.

"Connect your movements," she muttered under her breath like a mantra. "Grace, grace, grace, grace."

Nadia moved comfortably through her first dance pass. And she moved with more style than Kelly had ever seen in her routines. Nadia did a switch split into a triple turn at the corner of the floor. At the height of her aerial split, Nadia's legs were extended straight beyond 180 degrees, her toes pointed and her arms perfectly aligned, up and out. She landed millimeters from the edge, but she didn't step over, as if she had security sensors embedded in her heels.

The audience cheered wildly.

"Such a good sign!" Jamie said.

"She's killing it," added Raven.

Nadia must have felt their energy because each tumbling run was even higher and stronger than the last. Nadia shimmied into a step-ball-change before taking a deep breath in preparation for her next tumbling pass. She ran full-speed into a double-Arabian piked half out, turning into a backflip and twisting her body in the air. It was hard but Nadia made it look easy and graceful. The air itself seemed to be holding her up.

She paused in the corner for her last tumbling pass.

Kelley grabbed Jamie's hand.

Then Nadia ran full speed into a round-off, back handspring, back handspring, double back tuck.

She ended in a floor pose with her hands framing her face. Her legs were bent beneath her and her upper-body was strong. She collapsed onto the mat smiling, her chest moving up and down as she caught her breath.

"Nadia could so totally get into circus camp with that routine," Jamie joked.

Kelley slapped her.

"I'm so proud of you, Nadia!" she called as her friend walked off the mat. "You were positively regal!"

Nadia smiled. Her mom was up in the stands, but Nadia knew what she'd be saying if she were allowed on the floor. *You've already won a personal victory. Now go for the medal.*

The rest of the floor routines were also spectacular. The red-white-and-blue squad all pulled out solid performances, but it was Jamie's squad from Miami who stole the show, with one routine more fabulous than the last.

"Oh my god, they're like...professionals," Kelley said.

"Whatever," said Raven, "we're doing better than we've ever done in competition or practice. Comparing yourself to other teams is only going to shatter your confidence."

Raven was right. Each Kip put as much energy as possible into their floor routines as Nadia had. Jamie's was, as usual, the perfect blend of energy, artistry, and acro. She stepped out of a landing a little on a round-off costing her two-tenths of a point and she stepped out of bounds by a millimeter on her second tumbling pass which cost her another few tenths of a point, but otherwise, she performed well.

Kelley had not won Max over to her Beyonce song but had convinced him to mash-up her typical country music with a little bit of a hip hop beat and the unusual pairing had the audience on their feet and stomping along. For her second dance pass, he'd choreographed a unique combination of the running man and the do-si-do that even got a few people in the audience hooting and whistling.

"I think you actually like country music," Raven said as Kelley walked off the mat, her cheeks flushed and her eyes bright.

"Shh, don't tell Max," Kelley joked.

"Good performance, Kelley," said Nadia. "Steady. Solid."

Raven was up last and just knowing her parents were in the

audience put an extra bounce in her step that made her dance moves that much more dynamic and engaging. She swore she could even pinpoint her dad's voice cheering her on.

"That's my squad!" cried Max when they were all done.

The girls sat nervously as their scores came in. They were modest, but solid with Raven and Jamie scoring highest. Raven was only .5 of a point above Jamie.

I have to edge her out, Jamie thought, steeling her resolve to add in the new dismount. *I have to win back that tenth of a point in the next event.* She felt an instant pang of guilt. Raven was so nice to her. Why did Jamie want to beat her so badly? But competing against your friends and squad-mates was all part of gymnastics.

"I can't believe I stepped out on a round-off, though," complained Jamie.

"No stressing, Jamie," said Raven. "We'll make up that extra tenth of a percent on bars. Your scores are cumulative. We're looking at the big picture."

"Did you learn that from my mom?" Nadia asked.

"Sure did."

"She always does that. She said there's no need to look at scoring in a way that doesn't work for you. Beam is last. And we're going into it ahead. We don't have to be perfect. At least that's the theory."

"So there's not as much pressure," Kelley said.

"And you end up doing better than ever?" Jamie liked the philosophy.

"In theory," Nadia reminded them.

"So like—" Raven began.

"Okay, enough talking," said Nadia. "Let's do this."

"I'm proud of you girls," said Judi, sounding positive. "Keep it up."

"Okay, on to the next one," said Judi. "Wave to the crowd and head to the vault."

The vault competition was just as exciting. Each gymnast had to perform a salto vault with a tuck, pike or layout. One girl from New York almost scored a perfect ten.

"We'll have to look out for her," Nadia said.

Raven laughed. "What does that even mean? This isn't football. We can watch her all we want, but it's not like we can tackle her before she score or anything."

Raven winked at Nadia as she headed to the runway herself. She nodded to the judges in respect and then added an extra nod to Nadia before launching her body forward. She hit the springboard and propelled herself above the table with more energy than her squad had ever seen.

Her vault was near-perfect.

The audience and even Judi burst into applause.

"New girl has spirit," said Nadia.

Raven jogged off the mat, unable to hide how great she felt. She wrapped Nadia in a bear hug. "I was looking out for her. Did I do a good job?"

Nadia smiled.

"Your turn," said Raven.

The girls all pulled out solid vaults, including Kelley who had been having a hard time sticking her landings on her weak angles. There was a lot of force coming down out of a vault.

They all had the option of doing a second easier vault but every single Kip pulled out her toughest vault for the competition. And they all pulled them off more or less well.

"I've never seen Nadia get that much height on the Yurchenko with double full-twisting layout before," said Jamie.

"She tucked her butt in on the launch," said Raven. "Gave her so much extra height to play with."

"We are such a great team," Kelley said.

"And we've got the tracksuits to prove it," Jamie joked.

"What, these silver things?" Raven teased. "I don't know about you, but I'm going for gold. Hey, there's my old squad."

"Which ones?" Nadia said as she joined them, a little out of breath from her vault.

"The gold and royal blue track suits."

"Oh my god, that's the girl who did the Phelps at Regionals," said Jamie. "You know, the Tsukahara with a half-turn after the mount into a front layout."

"That vault was pretty sweet, Raven," called a freckled girl with red hair from Raven's old squad.

"Yeah, you should be competing with us," said another.

"I wish I could compete with you *and* the Kips," said Raven, "but there's not enough of me to go around."

"I hear that," her friend joked. Then she turned to the squad. "You guys look good out there. You're making us step up our game."

"Yeah," said the other girl. "Like my easiest tumbling pass almost didn't beat ALL yours in difficulty."

Then they walked off toward the beam for the next event.

The Kips grabbed their gear and headed toward the uneven bars for their next event. Beam would be last for their group.

Jamie's stomach fluttered with anxiety. She hadn't been able to practice her new dismount at the last practice—not with Judi watching. She'd tried in her bedroom at home, but the bed was just too bouncy to act as a stand-in for a beam.

"Kelly, how's that ankle?" Judi asked

"Nadia's mom wrapped it up this morning," Kelley said. "She's like amazing. I haven't even noticed it all day."

"I'm going to hire your mom fulltime, Nadia," Judi joked.

"Be careful what you wish for," Nadia said.

"It's good to see you smiling," Raven noticed.

"Don't push it Newbie," Nadia said.

"Miami, you're up."

The Kips had solid routines on uneven bars across the board with Nadia blowing them all away with her technical skills and Raven earning extra points for her unique dismount.

All the extra upper body training Kelley had been doing when she couldn't tumble on her ankle had really paid off. Her kips and handstands were really strong and straight. Her extension on every move was outstanding.

"Miami, you're up," Nadia called.

Jamie felt good going into beam, but she still really wanted to try something different. They were all doing so well. It seemed like a good moment to take the risk—to pull out the big moves.

Toward the end of her routine, Jamie mentally prepared to risk the new dismount. She tested her balance with her right foot like she always did.

This is where Judi is starting to freak out, Jamie thought.

Then Jamie hopped onto her right foot and kicked up with her left sending her body tilting up and next to the bar. But she didn't have enough momentum. She only managed to get one rotation in before she had to fight for the landing. It was an incredibly unspectacular dismount.

And Judi was steaming mad.

* * * * * * * * * * * * * * * * * * *

That night over dinner, the girls shared two plates of celebratory fries with their parents and coaches. They had all let their hair down and changed into jeans, but they still had hints of glitter on their eyelids and they were still wearing team colors. Nadia and Raven both had silver medals hanging around their necks.

"I'm just so proud of all of you," Judi said, looking at each of the girls in turn.

"What are the final standings exactly?" asked Jamie's mom.

"I placed paced second on bars," said Nadia, proudly.

She paused while the squad applauded and cheered for her.

"Our highest placement," Judi boasted on Nadia's behalf.

Raven leaned over and whispered in Nadia's ear. "It's okay to smile," she said. "You kicked butt."

Nadia's face broke into a big proud smile. "I did, didn't I?"

"It was amazing to watch," said Kelley. "You were like a rocket. Raven medaled, too. Second on vault."

"And you were an incredible mix of artistry and acro on beam, Kelley." Nadia turned to the group of parents. "Kelley placed sixth on beam and Jamie came in fourth, despite her bobbled dismount."

Jamie's cheeks flushed bright red, but she hooted and clapped anyway. Judi had given her a stern talking-to on the arena-floor, but she wasn't holding it against Jamie. Tonight was about celebrating.

"And I came in sixth on floor! Don't forget that one," said Jamie. "Only one place behind Raven."

Raven blushed. Her parents smiled at her proudly.

"I'd say it's all been very very worth it after all," her mom said.

"It would have been worth it if you hadn't placed at all," her dad added.

Raven looked around at her new squad, a happy mass of fuchsia, denim, and bright smiles. It had been a rough year, with the divorce and adjusting to a new squad and living in two homes. But seeing her new friends now—seeing the smiles on her parents' faces and the not-fighting they were doing—she had to admit that she thought it had all been worth it, too.

"I wouldn't trade this squad for anything," she said out loud. "Not for anything."

CHAPTER 17: GANGHAM KIP STYLE

The Kips all stood side by side on the edge of the hotel pool, wearing matching fuchsia bathing suits and sparkly silver clips in their hair. Nadia and Raven's silver medals decorating their necks.

"You got the remote?" Raven asked.

"Right here." Jamie held it up nervously.

"Cue music," said Kelley.

"I can't believe we're doing this," said Nadia. "This is so embarrassing."

"A deal's a deal," said Raven. She wrapped an arm around Jamie's shoulder. "And besides, we're a team and we all did well."

"All for one. And one for all," said Kelley.

"Hey, other squads," shouted Raven. "Are you ready for this?"

The mass of girls in the pool stopped what they were doing to look at the line-up of Kips. For a brief moment there was silence. Then the song, "Gangham Style" boomed over the pool's sound system. Everyone in the water started cheering as the Kips broke into lip sync complete with choreography.

Judi, Max, and Judi's friend got up off their lounge chairs to dance along.

Nadia even ad-libbed and started a can-can inspired kick line.

They made it half-way through before they all broke down into giggles and jumped into the water. Even Nadia.

Alex swam over with the rest of her squad and soon all the gymnast were splashing and singing along.

"Our first time at Nationals, squad," said Nadia, as she swam up beside Kelley.

"And we did really well," added Raven.

"Of course we did," said Jamie, wrapping her arms around her friends. "We're Kips."

ABOUT THE AUTHOR

April Adams has spent almost as much time upside down as right side up. As a competitive gymnast she led her University of Alabama team to the top of the podium and although her sights were never on the Olympics, after a degree in creative writing , April went as a journalist to the London games. April loves hiking, baking and spending time with her family in Utah.

17077918R00068

Made in the USA
Middletown, DE
26 November 2018